MS

Earl O. Heady

His Impact on Agricultural Economics

Earl O. Heady

His Impact on Agricultural Economics

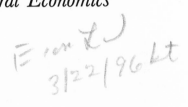

EDITED BY James Langley, Gary Vocke, & Larry Whiting

WITH ESSAYS BY   Raymond R. Beneke   Shashanka Bhide   Wilfred Candler

John L. Dillon   Marian Heady   Glenn L. Johnson   Leo V. Mayer

Donald O. Mitchell   William G. Murray   V. Nazarenko   Kenneth Nicol

John Pesek   Daryll E. Ray   Roland K. Roberts   Keith D. Rogers

Raymond Joe Schatzer   Lauren Soth   Luther Tweeten

Iowa State University Press / Ames

James Langley is Senior Policy Analyst, Agricultural Stabilization and Conservation Service, U.S. Department of Agriculture.

Gary Vocke is Agricultural Economist, Economic Research Service, U.S. Department of Agriculture.

Larry Whiting is Professor of Agricultural Education and Head, Department of Communication and Technology, College of Agriculture, The Ohio State University.

© 1994 Iowa State University Press, Ames, Iowa 50014

Authorization to photocopy items for internal or personal use, or the internal or personal use of specific clients, is granted by Iowa State University Press, provided that the base fee of $.10 per copy is paid directly to the Copyright Clearance Center, 27 Congress Street, Salem, MA 01970. For those organizations that have been granted a photocopy license by CCC, a separate system of payments has been arranged. The fee code for users of the Transactional Reporting Service is 0-8138-2249-1/94 $.10.

Printed on acid-free paper in the United States of America

First edition, 1994

FRONTISPIECE: Earl O. Heady (*Courtesy of Marian Heady*)

Library of Congress Cataloging-in-Publication Data
Earl O. Heady: his impact on agricultural economics / edited by James Langley, Gary Vocke & Larry Whiting.
    p.   cm.
Includes index.
ISBN 0-8138-2249-1
    1. Heady, Earl Orel. 2. Agricultural economists—United States—Biography. 3. Agriculture—Economic aspects. I. Langley, James A. II. Vocke, Gary. III. Whiting, Larry R.
    HD1771.5.H43E18 1994
    338.1′092—dc20
    [B]   94-5800

Contents

Preface   vii

Introduction   ix
Marian Heady

1. On Becoming "Distinguished"   3
   Raymond R. Beneke

2. Intellectual Breakthrough   24
   William G. Murray

3. Agricultural Sector Simulation Modeling   29
   Roland K. Roberts, Daryll E. Ray, Donald O. Mitchell, and Raymond Joe Schatzer

4. Agricultural Production-Function Analysis   52
   John L. Dillon

5. Isoclines and Isoquants: Expansion Paths and Substitution Rates   62
   John Pesek

6. Development and Application of Farm-level Programming Models
   and Other Farm Management Techniques   76
   Wilfred Candler

7. Applications of Linear Programming Techniques to
   Agricultural Sector Analysis   86
   Kenneth Nicol

8. Long-term Agricultural Development and Price and Income Policy   100
   Luther Tweeten and Leo V. Mayer

v

9. Income Compensation and Farm Supply Control   113
   Lauren Soth

10. The Science of Agricultural Economics in India: Implications
    of Heady's Contributions   118
    Shashanka Bhide

11. Soviet Research into the Use of Economic and Mathematical
    Methods in Agriculture   127
    V. Nazarenko

12. Impact on a Nation: The Professor, the Students, and the Institutions 131
    Keith D. Rogers

13. Two Reviews of *Economics of Agricultural Production and Resource Use*   158
    Glenn L. Johnson

Appendix: A Personal Synopsis   193

N A

Preface

This book relates Dr. Earl O. Heady's contributions to the development of the science of agricultural economics and describes the extent of his efforts to promote the application of science to solving real world problems. After the introductory essay by Marian Heady, professional colleagues comment on various subject areas in which Dr. Heady worked, both domestic and foreign. They indicate how he was able to work with others in multidisciplinary research efforts to solve real world problems; how he trained students from around the world; and how his work continues to be both a foundation and inspiration for future generations of economists. These accounts provide both a personal and a professional view of Dr. Heady's activities.

The book concludes with a reprint of two critical reviews of Dr. Heady's *Economics of Agricultural Production and Resource Use*. The purpose of these reprints is to recognize the long-lasting influence of this book on agricultural economic analysis from the independent perspective of a distinguished contemporary of Dr. Heady.

During Dr. Heady's long and prolific career at Iowa State University, he authored or co-authored 26 books and 750 journal articles, research bulletins, and other professional papers. He guided the graduate school research of over 300 students. Each of these students made important contributions to the body of empirical work associated with Dr. Heady's career.

This book was conceived and managed by James Langley, Gary

Vocke, and Larry Whiting. We appreciate each author's willingness to undertake the task of preparing original chapters that address particular aspects of their experiences with Dr. Heady. Taken together, the chapters provide a prospective on how one individual was able to develop a very successful academic career and how, as Emery Castle stated, "we can all see farther because we can stand on his shoulders."

We especially thank Marian Heady for her permission and encouragement in preparing this book. Dr. Raymond Beneke provided unending support for the project. Iowa State University Press provided invaluable assistance. Many other students and colleagues of Dr. Heady expressed considerable support, interest, and understanding throughout the course of this project, for which we are grateful.

We greatly appreciate the generous financial support for publishing this book from the Earl O. Heady Appreciation Club of the American Agricultural Economics Association Foundation. Any profits from the sale of this book will go to the Appreciation Club to help further the legacy of our distinguished and beloved professor, colleague, and friend, Dr. Earl O. Heady.

MARIAN HEADY

Introduction

E arl O. Heady generated respect professionally and personally. He was soft-spoken, humble, and compassionate and had a subtle sense of humor, a ready smile, and many stories to tell. It was true that he worked long and hard hours, often until 2:00 or 2:30 a.m., but he always gave generously of his time to his wife, three children, and three grandchildren. He was extremely thoughtful.

Whenever he traveled, our first bit of correspondence came the next day from the airport in Chicago. He wrote detailed letters to the family each day he was away. For many years, until there was no longer space on the map, we recorded his travels on a large world map; this gave us a feeling that he was with us as well as an excellent geography lesson and ample table conversation. His discipline was firm but he never raised his voice or a hand. His calm, mild manner transferred to his counseling of graduate students and his participation with his colleagues.

Earl Heady was modest, reserved, and fair. He didn't deviate when he thought he was right; he'd fight to the end for his convictions. He was always bursting with ideas for research, books and articles, and for ways to improve the quality of life for those in agriculture. He had a phenomenal power of concentration. Many lectures, papers, and chapters of books were written in airports and on airplanes. Every bit of writing he did was in longhand. He would write, have the material typed, revise, and have the second draft typed. It was typical for him to revise three or four times. When asked what the necessary ingredient was to being such a prolific writer, he'd respond, "You just put a little glue on the seat of your pants."

He was a hard taskmaster. He disciplined himself to work hard, and he expected his graduate students and colleagues to do the same. Heady graduate students were always in high demand because they were well trained. Many hold important positions in the United States and abroad. Heady students throughout the world are proud to have been his students. Students of his graduate students have proudly told me they were Dr. Heady's grandchildren.

For a better understanding of the forces that developed his work ethic, I give you a bit of his early biography.

Earl O. Heady was born January 25, 1916, on his parents' farm seven miles from the tiny western Nebraska town of Champion. He was the sixth of eight children. With four older sisters to help inside the home, he was soon relegated to such outside chores as gathering corn cobs for the cook stove and cleaning the horse stalls. At age eleven he asked his father when he'd be old enough to work in the fields; he envied his older brother who had been working with his father for three or four years. His father promptly and quietly hitched up two of the horses and a plow and told him to go to work. Thus began his life of hard work and long hours. His favorite recollection of those days was the time of rest at the end of two corn rows when he absorbed a great deal of his father's philosophy. It was during one of these times that his father said, "Get all the education you can; it's something they can't take away from you." Earl was never sure who "they" were, but he took the suggestion seriously.

From the one-room school house with various seventeen- and eighteen-year-old teachers having a mere normal training education in high school, he learned his lessons well — so well that midway through eighth grade the young teacher told him to stay home, do whatever he wanted, and study for the eighth grade examinations. It was during this time that he read a set of encyclopedias from cover to cover.

He attended and graduated from high school in Imperial, Nebraska, living in town during the week and thus managing his own time and activities. He channeled his extra time to sports: he was quarterback on the football team all four of his high school years. As a freshman he weighed just ninety-seven pounds. He played every minute of every game, calling all plays. Imperial had champion teams during those years.

The depression necessitated his working on the farm one year before he entered the University of Nebraska in 1934. When he left for the university, his only new item of clothing was a suit. His father slipped fifty dollars in the pocket. Tuition was twenty-five dollars a semester, so it didn't leave him much to spend frivolously. He was self-supporting as a student, working chiefly in the Agronomy Department during the school year and in agronomy test plots in the summer. He and another fraternity brother earned their room and board by preparing breakfast and doing the dishes afterward at the Alpha Gamma Rho house. He had a double major, agricultural economics and agronomy, when he obtained his Bachelor of Science degree in 1938. He completed his Master's of Science degree in agricultural economics at the University of Nebraska in 1939. He was elected to many honorary organizations, was on judging teams, and held offices in numerous campus organizations and his fraternity. The pace had been set.

One year of work for the Federal Land Bank in Omaha and in York County, Nebraska, convinced him that he preferred to be in academic work. He applied to Iowa State College and became an instructor in agricultural economics in September 1940. While teaching full time, he pursued his Ph.D. degree, usually carrying twelve hours each quarter; he completed his doctorate in 1945. He was appointed a full professor in 1949, having already developed a strong research program with a large graduate student following.

He was frequently offered opportunities at other institutions. Iowa State always surpassed these offers and continuously gave him freedom to do whatever he wished. He never short-changed Iowa State; throughout his career he did the work of two or three people.

Earl was a history buff and spent many hours reading history books. He had a photographic memory and remembered everything he read. Also because of his great memory he always knew where each of his 359 former graduate students were, their positions, and the projects on which they were working. He was as proud of each graduate student as he was of his own children.

His chief hobby was Heady family genealogy. Together we'd been on every piece of land his ancestors had farmed and in all of the relevant cemeteries from Egg Harbor, New Jersey, to western Nebraska. He and a second cousin published a "Heady Family Quarterly Newsletter" for four years; these are found in the Library of Congress. He also was a gardener and took great pride in a weedless lawn.

Excerpts from letters from two of his former colleagues complement what I've written. Dr. C. C. Maji, a former graduate student and now Assistant Director-General of the Indian Center for Agricultural Research in New Delhi, India, wrote,

> Dr. Heady was an extraordinary economist of our time with an outstanding and unsurpassable professional attainment. In fact, he was an institution in himself with hundreds of his direct students working in responsible positions all over the globe. Above all, he was one of the most compassionate, understanding and kind-hearted persons I have ever known. . . . His values, ideals and sweet memories will live in me till my last days and will inspire me to live in search of excellence.

A former secretary, Cathy Jacobson Ahrenholz, wrote,

> How wonderful to have lived the life Dr. Heady lived and to leave such a rich heritage. Those of us privileged to have worked with him were given an opportunity few people are rarely given. I feel the learning experiences I had working for Dr. Heady far outweigh many college degrees. He will always remain in my mind as first of all a gentleman, soft-spoken, patient, understanding and caring for people. He knew how he wanted things completed and then trusted the completion to us, his secretaries. He always tackled things with a positive approach. In all the years I knew him, not once did he show that he was angry or upset with us. I know we gave him cause at times. . . .
> He was a brilliant man, sharing his knowledge with the world. However, with all of his talents, teaching, the many books he wrote, the students he supervised and his travels, his family and home were nearest and dearest to him.

The quotation from the *Des Moines Register* on the bronze plaque in Heady Hall, the Iowa State University building dedicated to him in 1982, expresses his accomplishments well:

Few have done so much

to improve the well-being of so many

throughout the world.

Earl Heady is respected for his writings, his research, his training of graduate students and, perhaps greatest of all, for his humanitarianism.

Earl O. Heady

His Impact on Agricultural Economics

RAYMOND R. BENEKE

———————

1

On Becoming "Distinguished"

M y objectives are (1) to attempt to identify the forces both from the outside and from within that propelled Professor Heady to enormous achievement and thus to worldwide eminence; (2) to provide insight into the manner in which Heady's early efforts gained momentum step by step and blossomed ultimately into a unique and spectacular career; and (3) to give those who participated as students, colleagues, supporters, and admirers a clearer picture of the early years.

THE INGREDIENTS OF A DISTINGUISHED CAREER

Exogenous Factors

I want first to cite exogenous factors over which Earl had little control that enabled the snowball first to begin to form and then to develop into an avalanche of achievement in four decades of professional activity.

———————

Raymond R. Beneke is Professor Emeritus, Department of Economics, Iowa State University.

1. The timing of Professor Heady's birth was propitious in that he reached maturity at a time when economics was undergoing a revolution. In the two decades preceding Earl's entry into graduate school, economics had undergone a major transformation. The theory of a competitive economy in equilibrium at full employment was called into question by the events of the early twentieth century. In addition, the marginal analysis of Marshall looked much like an application of differential calculus to mathematicians. A few of the latter began to trickle into the profession in the 1920s and 1930s. There had also had been major developments in statistics. The mix of economists with a background in mathematics and the new breed of statistician led to the development of econometrics—the application of economics and statistical theory to economic problems and data sets. These tools had been developed and were waiting for Earl when he entered the profession.

2. Thus, Earl's entry into economics in the late 1930s was well timed. His choice of Iowa State as a place for advanced study in 1940 also proved to be fortunate for a student of his talents and aspirations. Twenty years earlier E. G. Nourse, a young Ph.D. out of the University of Chicago, molded and then fought to retain a Department of Economics which integrated agricultural economics and general economics into a single unit.[1] By 1940 economics at Iowa State was under the leadership of the brilliant and aggressive T. W. Schultz, who had both the propensity and talent for recruiting bright young economists—both agricultural and general—on to his staff. He had the capacity to motivate both the new recruits and the veterans to great efforts. When Earl came to Iowa State Gerhard Tinter, William Nichols, A. G. Hart, Geoffrey Shepard, and William Murray were there waiting for him. Later, after Heady had finished his degree, Ken Boulding, and Leonard Hurwitz joined the staff.

3. While Schultz was building an incomparably productive team of economists and agricultural economists, George Snedecor was developing a creative, talented, and highly motivated team of young statisticians. In 1933 the Iowa State Statistical Laboratory emerged out of Snedecor's vision and creativity; it had a major purpose of reaching out to aid other disciplines in the application of the new statistics. Most graduate students in economics took minor degrees in statistics. Indeed they often complained that they spent more time

studying statistics than economics. Paul Homeyer, Ray Jessen, and Cliff Hildreth—all three contemporary students with Heady and all with strong training in economics—became staff members in statistics. This trio interacted regularly with Heady during the mid-1940s. T. A. Bancroft and H. O. Hartley also worked jointly with Earl in the late forties. Earl Heady learned a great deal from these people and often remarked that he learned more statistics when he worked with them than he ever did in the classroom.

4. When Earl arrived in Ames, Iowa State had a well established tradition of excellence in agricultural economics. Henry C. Taylor, who more than any other person had established agricultural economics as a discipline, studied for his master's degree at Iowa State in 1898. B. H. Hibbard taught agricultural economics there in the early 1900s. By 1940, work in the discipline was well supported, and under the leadership of T. W. Schultz was staffed with talented people. In 1944 Schultz became disenchanted with Iowa State administrators over issues of academic freedom surrounding economic studies analyzing the role of dairy production in a wartime economy and left ISU. There began with Schultz's departure a mass exodus of tenured staff members from the Economics Department. This resulted in areas of research and teaching being thinly staffed and, more importantly, in already-funded research projects being left without staff or leadership. Earl, even as a beginning participant in the competition for funding, was quick to recognize the opportunities this situation presented.

Endogenous Factors

Now I turn to the endogenous factors, those that Earl brought to the scene himself which, in my view, contributed to his distinguished career.

1. Earl's first love was agriculture. He grew up on a farm in Western Nebraska during an era when farming was an arduous lifestyle, working hours were long, and returns for one's efforts were meager. Although hard work and lower returns were characteristic of pioneer life on the frontier of agriculture, it was doubly true while Earl was growing up due to the Great Depression and the chronic

drought of the early thirties. Earl had a firsthand knowledge of most
farm operations and had experienced the hardships and the pleasures
that go with working with plants, animals, and machines. He had a
genuine interest in agriculture and spoke always with nostalgia about
his early days on the farm. As an undergraduate he majored in
agriculture. This understanding and interest in animal and plant
science and in agricultural engineering contributed greatly to his cred-
ibility when it came time to seek out scientists in technical agriculture
to participate in joint projects. Contrary to what colleagues and students often deduced, Earl had no deep interest in mathematics and
had only a basic knowledge of algebra and calculus when he began his
graduate studies. I have a copy of R. D. G. Allen's *Mathematics for
Economists* which Earl used as a graduate student and referred to often
during his early work as a professional. The book is crammed with
notes, reminders, and explanations which he had made for himself.

Earl often commented that it was necessary to know only a
limited amount of mathematics, statistics, and economics to be an
effective economic analyst. But he insisted that it was of great importance to understand thoroughly what you did know in these areas.
Earl came to Iowa State in 1940 as an instructor in principles. The
standard teaching load was four sections, each meeting three times
per week. He arranged his schedule to teach four hours in a row from
8:00 to 12:00 on Monday, Wednesday, and Friday mornings, leaving
the afternoons and Tuesdays and Thursdays free for study and research. In spite of the repetition, Earl contended that each time
through the material he always understood his subject matter a little
more thoroughly. He taught from a textbook written by Bowman and
Bach entitled *Economic Analysis and Public Policy,* which first appeared in
1943 and continued for many years as a widely used principles text.
He had known both Bowman and Bach while they were on the staff at
Iowa State and was fond of this book all the rest of his life. Earl
sometimes remarked that the reason some advanced students ran into
difficulty on more complex relationships was that their knowledge of
the fundamentals was not sufficiently thorough. He looked upon undergraduate teaching as important in the training of advanced students and encouraged his students to teach if the opportunity arose
during their graduate training.

2. Earl brought to his work optimism and a well-founded appre-

ciation of his own talents and capacity to get things done. He was self-reliant, disciplined, and persevering. These are traits one imagines were born out of the struggles of life on a western Nebraska farm during the Great Depression and droughts of the 1930s.

3. Earl had an unusual talent for establishing rapport with students, and he excelled in working with small groups or on a one-on-one basis. He did not delude himself that he was a mover and shaker in the classroom. During his early years when he was just beginning to make his mark he conducted a rotating seminar with students as they made their way back and forth from the Agricultural Annex to the Memorial Union twice a day for coffee. It was then that he shared what was on his mind with students and vice versa. That was during the era when he supervised perhaps ten or a dozen active graduate students. In retrospect he attracted a remarkably able group in the late 1940s and early 1950s even though he was young and new to the profession. Most of them went on to distinguished careers as professional agricultural economists[2] or academic administrators. Ideas flowed freely and it was a two-way process — students gave Earl their perspectives and challenged and defined more sharply his thinking. At this stage of his career Earl was working with graduate students who were essentially his same age, most being recently returned veterans of World War II. While students of this era respected Earl's talent and dedication, none stood in awe of him. Later as his reputation grew, the age differences increased, and as Earl became more involved professionally this easy camaraderie fell by the wayside. It is no exaggeration to report that later generations of students did stand in awe of Professor Heady. When the numbers grew to forty or fifty graduates, time with him, even for those who were in the midst of dissertations and funded research projects, was much more severely rationed. Although he made Herculean efforts to overcome the problem, the lack of time and guidance were a frequent complaint.

The capacity to attract graduate students at the early stages of his career was largely a function of his ability to make believers out of those with whom he was working. They were his recruiters and encouraged and sometimes urged friends and colleagues to join the throng that was studying with Heady. He accepted each student as his responsibility and he sensed that his concern for them magnified their talents and kindled their intellectual growth. He was loyal to them—

too loyal at times — and his loyalty begat their loyalty. It was in teaching students to do research, to define and analyze problems, and then to report the results of their efforts by presenting them in an intelligible form that Earl was at his best. Lack of confidence in what they are doing and what they have written often leads to a crisis in the careers of advanced degree aspirants. Indeed, many fail to complete the degree primarily because of a lack of courage and motivation. All of this Earl understood well. He also knew that fortune favors the brave and that success is the child of audacity, and he was a master at communicating this spirit to struggling students. In the early years Heady attempted to have several one-on-one sessions per month with students actively pursuing research and writing. These sessions, designed to serve as tonics to students, were typically brief with student and professor reviewing materials that the student had earlier provided. Regardless of how miserable the efforts of the student had been, Earl would always find something positive to build on, although in some cases doing so required more than a little searching. As a result, the student left the encounter rejuvenated and ready for more work. Because he combined skill in motivating young people with perseverance and with superlative imagination and talent, Earl saw a high proportion of his students complete their degrees.

    4. Earl was goal oriented. As he was completing his Ph.D. he had already laid out a surprisingly detailed blueprint of what he proposed to do with his talents. He had sufficient imagination to dream tall dreams, and he did. He foresaw how he would change the orientation of research in farm management and production economics in 1946 and laid out the plan in an 1948 article in the *Journal of Farm Economics*.[3] At this stage he had not yet discovered the underdeveloped countries; this awakening would come a few years later. Like many of his day, Professor Heady saw plenty that needed improvement in the domestic economy. He had no doubt that modern economic analysis had an enormous contribution to make to the human race. He knew he could make a difference and was determined to do so. The first problem was to train adequate numbers of people to do the research and teaching that needed to be done.

ORGANIZING FOR ACTION

At the beginning of his career Professor Heady foresaw that he would need a task force of helpers to accomplish all that he already had on his agenda. He looked upon graduate assistants as the primary source of professional assistance during the late 1940s and early 1950s. Later he developed the pattern of one or more tenure track positions filled by recent Ph.D.'s and several postdoctoral positions. Although Earl attracted primarily able graduate students, he would accept and tolerate some who were lacking in ability and/or motivation. He knew he was not allocating his own talent and energy efficiently when he tried to mold "tag-enders" into first-rate economists. They were the ones who required the most attention and certainly the greatest input of his time for what they accomplished. This group also caused him the greatest grief because out of loyalty he was inclined to come to their defense when they became mired in academic difficulty with little real prospect of survival. He was led into this trap partly because of his faith in the capacity of young people to grow. It was always difficult for him to say no to a prospective student. Perhaps of greater importance than either of these factors was that once his program gathered momentum there were always funds available to accommodate one more assistant. And there was always more territory to conquer than his existing army could subdue and occupy. In later years it was not unusual for him to have forty or fifty students in residence at one time. We talked on several occasions about the advantages of cutting the number in half and increasing the postdoctoral component of his brigade. He could never bring himself to cut back on students but comforted himself with the prospect that he would be getting out of the graduate student business altogether when he reached 70. I doubt that Earl would have been comfortable with life without students, but he did yearn for fewer hassles in his later years and hassles often came to him in the form of problems his graduate students were experiencing. When Heady accepted students into his group he felt responsible for supporting them financially until they finished their degrees. Because he never was certain that the funds would continue to flow, he maintained a reserve from which to meet his soft money obligations to students and contractors. In time the accumulation grew to substantial dimensions. In 1983 he told me he had reserves of sufficient magnitude to meet all of his obligations, i.e., he could see all of his current crop of graduate students through to their degrees. He confided on this occasion that the prospect of accepting no more students was inviting and he resolved to do just that. But when the applications for admission actually arrived, he could not resist the temptation to urge new prospects to join his team.

Earl was firmly convinced that you learned to do research by on-the-job training. He sought to assign students a role on a project the first day they arrived in Ames. Typically in later years he worked out a hierarchy of responsibility wherein a near Ph.D. or a postdoctoral staff member was in charge of a project and supervised several veteran students. The veteran students in turn would supervise the neophytes. Professor Heady kept in remarkably close touch with the progress of each project although doing so at times pushed him to the limit. Before any major trips, and there were many, he dictated long memos providing suggestions and instructions concerning the manner in which work was to proceed in his absence.

Given the magnitude of the research effort that he had mounted, the bottleneck in the operation was a chronic shortage of field generals—talented postdoctoral and tenure track staff who could substitute for Earl in leadership roles. By the time they had been in the system for six or eight years—and in some cases for eight to ten years—these young men were highly trained economists capable of running their own shows. Invariably they were not given the responsibility for planning and budget and the degree of recognition that they thought appropriate. It was the familiar scene of the father not recognizing that his offspring had arrived at full maturity. The young men selected to serve as Heady field generals were highly competent and well motivated. Consequently their services were in demand by other organizations, so inevitably they left the Heady operation for attractive alternatives. Parting was not easy for either the young professor or for Earl, but wives typically thought the break represented a liberation and that their spouse in the future would be home evenings—something that rarely happened while their husbands were part of Heady's team. Invariably Earl felt privately that the departed had ordered their professional priorities incorrectly, but in the years following their departure he followed their careers closely and took pride in their professional accomplishments.

THE RESEARCH AGENDA OF THE FIRST DECADE

Professor Heady's first major treatise on the pattern which farm management and production economics research should take was published in the May 1948 issue of the *Journal of Farm Economics*. At the time Earl published this article, he had completed his graduate study and had been appointed to a tenure track position as assistant professor at Iowa State University, where he was charged with revitalizing the farm management teaching and research program. This was a time of change, growth, optimism, and great opportunity for a young staff member in the Department of Economics at Iowa State because most of the old hands had left for greener pastures.

This remarkable journal article summarized what a brilliant student had digested from five years of interacting with a high-quality faculty and highly motivated colleagues. One also sees in it the influence of several writers whom Earl admired and often quoted in those first years. A thorough understanding of the theory of the firm is manifest in the article, no doubt in part a product of many hours in the classroom teaching from Bowman and Bach. Also evident is the influence of a little-known book by Melvin Reder entitled *Studies in the Theory of Welfare Economics* (New York: Columbia University Press, 1947). Earl also recommended that students interested in welfare economics read the works of Oskar Lange, including *On the Economic Theory of Socialism* (New York: McGraw-Hill, 1938).

The 1948 article presented a "classification of the specific problems of individual farms as business units. The economic concepts which provide the theoretical answer or hypothesis about the nature and kind of data and the design of the sample appropriate if the problems are to be answered are included in parentheses" (p. 202).

1. The level of output to be attained from (or the rate of input applied to) fixed or specialized resources. (Diminishing returns and equation of marginal [additional] cost and revenue.)

2. The combination of enterprises within a given time period. (Marginal rates of factor substitution, product contours and equation of productivities and costs of resources.)

3. The combination of enterprises within a given time period. (Marginal rates of transformation, equation of marginal returns in vari-

ous alternatives or proportionality of prices and marginal rates of product substitution.)

4. The timing of production (sales) given certainty (near) as to
price variation — the problem of seasonal price variations. (A special
case of problem 3 with the output of a given commodity in two different
time periods taking on the same relationships as the output of two
commodities at a given point in time.)

5. The level of resource conservation. (A special consideration of
problem 1 with a different time span consideration and including considerations of time preference and interest rates.)

6. The optimum scale of operation. (Returns to scale and short-
run and long-run cost curves; equation of marginal costs and returns,
capital rationing, returns discounting, and risk aversion.)

7. The method of obtaining control of the resources to be used in
production and the consequent combination of resources. (Equity ratios
and principles of increasing risk, resource productivities and market
prices for factors, price and production uncertainties and discounting of
future returns.)

8. Adjusting to change and uncertainty of the market and production process including growth of the business over time. (Probability
distributions, discounting returns, flexibility and adaptability of the enterprise, timing of production and dispersion and convergence of expected prices.)

The problems set forth in this statement constituted a research
agenda which Heady was to follow during the next decade.[4] To a
major degree it also anticipated the organization and content of the
blue book, *Economics of Agricultural Production and Resource Use* (Englewood Cliffs, N.J.: Prentice Hall, 1952).

The late 1940s and early 1950s were devoted to pursuing the
above agenda. All of the topics listed received attention in one form or
another. A pattern typically followed was for Earl to team up with a
graduate student in exploring a problem on which to focus and together fashioning a method for analyzing it. Earl learned along with
the student. Among the first problems to attract Heady's energies was
the matter of optimum level of production and the optimum combination of resources. These early efforts took the form of attempting
empirically to estimate the production surface in a variety of crop and
livestock production activities. The earliest evidence of participation
in this type of activity is represented by a Master of Science thesis
prepared by Lee Day[5] under Earl's supervision. The project repre-

sented an attempt to estimate marginal rates of substitution between corn and protein in pork production. This early interest grew out of the environment that existed in the land-grant colleges during that period. Recommendations being made by agricultural scientists to farm producers often were criticized by the latter because they sometimes ignored dollars and cents implications. For the most part, plant and animal scientists fell back upon such questionable criteria as maximizing yield per acre, achieving maximum rate of gain, or achieving a balanced return. The world was ready for more sophisticated decision-making rules, and Professor Heady was enthusiastic about providing information more appropriate for defining project maximization or cost minimization guides. Making progress on this front was a tedious business because experimental design in the plant and animal sciences was oriented toward providing evidence to compare which practice among a set provided the greatest physical response. R. A. Fisher's analysis of variance models were in vogue and were deeply ingrained in the minds of the agricultural scientists of the day. The parameters which Heady was attempting to estimate fundamentally involved an exercise in regression analysis and required modifications in conventional experimental design for reasonable results. Earl gradually interested several agricultural scientists in his approach and published extensively on production functions during the first half of his career.[6] This was the arena in which most of his interdisciplinary work was to take place.[7]

In 1948 Heady published an article on the choice of crop enterprises.[8] The 1948 work, along with Harold Jensen's dissertation, was the extent of his involvement in enterprise selection until he began to apply linear programming. His first major involvement with linear programming as an analytical tool was in supervising the Ph.D. thesis of Bernard Bowlen (1954) although he published an article explaining to the profession the logic of linear programming in 1954.[9] Several articles on the use of linear programming preceded Heady's efforts in the area.[10] Although Earl was not a pioneer in this area, he saw clearly that the technique held great promise in adding rigor to enterprise choice and farm organization. In the early 1950s the major obstacle to the realistic application of linear programming to farm planning was the enormous calculating burden its use imposed upon the user. Although the computer was invented at Iowa State, it was not among the early institutions to have such a device installed and functioning.

By the mid-1950s the intense interest Heady had developed in the area of production functions and applications of linear programming to farm planning was limited by the computational time required. Regression analysis with several variables and large data sets such as those involved in animal nutrition could take weeks of work, especially if one sought a high degree of confidence in the accuracy of the regression estimates. The same was true of applications involving linear programming to farm planning. The illustrations that were being cranked out on farm enterprise selection on hand calculators were of such limited scope as to have no practical value. Professor Heady yearned for access to the electronic computing capabilities that were beginning to appear in selected universities. The University of Illinois had ILLIAC, a home engineered and constructed facility which was being used occasionally by agricultural economists at the University of Illinois. Iowa State undertook the construction of a facility patterned after the ILLIAC, drawing upon personnel who had participated in the Illinois project. Construction of the new computing facility, labelled the Cyclone, was a long and tedious process but it offered hope that someday soon computational capacity would no longer be a bottleneck.

While the Cyclone construction project was under way IBM presented the 650 to the world. Heady was resolved to have one at Iowa State. With the strong support of George Browning[11] and working with T. A. Bancroft, Heady convinced the administration to install a 650 in the fall of 1956. Bancroft, as director of the computer project, hired H. O. Hartley and Dale Grosvenor to develop software to accommodate potential users of the 650. Grosvenor recalls that Heady and his group were heavy users of the new facility and one of the principal users of the linear programming software they were developing. The initial configuration with appropriate software could accommodate a matrix of ninety-eight rows. The number of variables was flexible and, with a patient and ingenious operator, could be expanded to several hundred. Capacity of this magnitude meant that farm planning models with sufficient restraints and activities to permit useful results could be optimized. It was not long, however, as models were refined and made more sophisticated, before the capacity of the computer facility became limiting. In 1959 the 650 was upgraded so that it could accommodate 198 rows and many more variables. The immediate impact upon economics was to make linear programming a feasible tool for analyzing a wide range of problems. While the computer made linear programming feasible as an analytical tool, it reduced the cost of regression analysis in a spectacular way. Heady once commented to me that the 650 had made regression analysis a free service compared with the old days. As a result, new families of exotic regression models came on the scene to tempt researchers to look at the data from new directions. Earl and his students enjoyed proliferating the regression equation forms they fitted to data sets. Readers of their work sometimes complained that they were confronted with more results than they could interpret[12] and accused the authors of substituting multiple alternative outcomes for critical judgment.

Inter-Regional Models

As far back as 1945, when I first knew Dr. Heady, he had a strong interest in regional economics and was keenly interested in what many colleagues found a tedious question: why are agricultural commodities produced where they are? When the IBM 650 became operational, Earl began to experiment with linear programming applications to inter-regional competition. Because he quickly discovered that even the expanded IBM 650 lacked the capacity to accommodate a realistic analysis of competition among regions, Earl continued to pressure the computer center to expand its capacity. By 1962 he had arranged for use of computer facilities of the Standard Oil Company of New Jersey to optimize large regional models which Al Egbert was then developing. The work on regional models soon was modified to provide insight into policy questions, and for the next twenty years Earl devoted much time and effort to increasing the relevance, the range, and the scope of regional models with policy implications. In later years the modeling activity was extended still further to include an international dimension. The age of computers overlapped the last thirty years of Professor Heady's life. During that period computers and computer software steadily increased in speed, capacity, and sophistication, but Earl never worked with a computing system he considered adequate to his needs because until the end, larger and more sophisticated models were constantly gestating in his mind.

THE ORIGINS OF CARD

During the mid-1950s the American agriculture sector was suffering acute symptoms from its chronic ailment of overcapacity. A group of agricultural leaders who had been friends of Iowa State for many years met on several occasions to discuss new approaches to an old problem. At the same time, several faculty members at ISU who were deeply concerned about the difficulties confronting Corn Belt agriculture were discussing among themselves what the university might do to provide leadership in finding solutions to the dilemma. The idea of a center focused on research and education in agricultural adjustment emerged from joint discussions between the two groups. The idea of a major new and expanded effort in the policy area originated with Professors Donald Kaldor, Wallace Ogg, and Geoffrey Shephard. Those three and the off-campus leaders were urging more emphasis on policy questions on the part of the university.

Although until this point Heady had focused his attention upon the economics of farm production and was involved only peripherally in the area of conventional agricultural policy, he readily agreed to support the initiative. Earl had confided to me earlier on several occasions that he hoped to have a significant impact in policy research after he had established a solid base in production economics. Heady was a useful ally in the effort to develop a focus in policy research because he had worked with James Hilton while the latter was Dean of Agriculture at North Carolina State University, where Earl had spent a semester while on leave from Iowa State. Heady was a strong Hilton supporter both before and after Hilton became President of Iowa State, and he had Hilton's respect and support. With President Hilton's help the group obtained a special appropriation in 1958 from the Iowa General Assembly to establish a Center for Agricultural Adjustment. The grant was administered by the Dean of Agriculture, Floyd Andre, who looked upon the center as an interdisciplinary instrument and allocated parts of the added funds to the major departments in the college.

Because the support was fragmented, the center had no visible impact on research activities in the college. Those responsible for the center idea felt a sense of betrayal as they watched the funds for the center siphoned away to support more conventional research in agronomy and animal science. In its first year the center existed only on paper and constituted an additional budget line from which traditional programs could draw sustenance. This approach created a good deal of unhappiness both on and off the campus by those who had quite different aspirations for the center. It was not an effective organization during its early years.

After several years of frustration, Heady took the leadership in developing a grant proposal to bring additional funds to the campus which could be used for programs in general policy research and education. He succeeded in obtaining a grant of $448,500 from the W. K. Kellogg Foundation in 1962 to extend over a five-year period. To avoid a replay of the previous frittering away process, a condition of the grant was that Heady would have a major voice in the way the funds were used.

After the initial year or two, the head of economics was assigned the responsibility for the administration of CARD with Heady as the coordinator who in turn was to work with an advisory committee. His colleagues, trying to help steer the enterprise in the direction they thought it should move, discovered that in these matters Earl's was the only vote that counted. Other staff members in the department gradually dropped out of center activities and Earl developed his own staff of graduate students and postdoctoral personnel. From the beginning until Earl's incapacitation CARD nominally was an entity within the Department of Economics. As a practical matter, Heady sought and was accorded great autonomy both within the department and the college. On substantive matters, in his later years, he interacted directly with the vice president for finance and the president of the university when he felt it advantageous to do so.

Changing Labels for CARD

We digress now for a brief explanation of the labels that have been attached to the center over the years. As nearly as I can discern the name changes, although numerous, reflected no substantive shift in function. The evolution of names was as follows:

1958   Center for Agricultural Adjustment
1960   Center for Agricultural and Economic Adjustment
1962   Center for Agricultural and Economic Development
1971   Center for Agricultural and Rural Development

Whatever the original purposes of the center, it in fact became a vehicle for accommodating the broad, ambitious, and shifting research program of Heady's. Center activities reflected Earl's interests at the time and the funding he was able to attract. After the first decade, funds for economic development work became an important item in the center's budget.

During the years of Heady's leadership, CARD was the container in which one man's research efforts were packaged. It provided an entity around which the young people laboring on Earl's projects could rally and develop an esprit de corps. As the years progressed the group gradually became an organization with an identity separate from the Department of Economics and it constituted a device by which Earl could identify his turf and hence discourage encroachment by his colleagues.

Although the center probably served Earl well for public relations purposes and in attracting funding, it also created problems for him. In spite of the efforts both Earl and his students made to set the operation apart from the department, the limits to doing so were severe and unyielding. Most of the personnel in CARD were students interested in obtaining advanced degrees. CARD had no degree-granting authority and hence Earl's students were confronted ultimately with meeting department and university standards. On occasion Heady and his students did not agree with the faculty in the Department of Economics on what constituted appropriate standards for the Ph.D. dissertation and for performance on examinations. In those cases the views of the faculty prevailed.

In another major area Earl's passion for separateness caused him and his proteges problems. The center had no provisions for granting tenure since it functioned largely with soft money and was not recognized as a separate academic department. Thus as Earl sought to tenure members of the center staff he sometimes encountered problems. Tenure in the Department of Economics required an affirmative vote of the faculty in economics, a prerogative which the department guarded with zeal. This was not a matter of spite nor hostility toward Heady. Earl's relations with the staff were remarkably civil and cordial given the areas for misunderstanding and tension that his operation entailed. But there were a number of cases in which Earl and the faculty differed in appraising his candidates and the rejection which followed was always a traumatic experience for Earl.

One can easily exaggerate the importance of the center in shaping and facilitating Earl's career. It came on the scene after the Heady career was well established. On balance, his contribution would probably have been substantially the same without it and he would have been spared an enormous burden of housekeeping chores and a good many hassles with his colleagues.

INTERNATIONAL ACTIVITIES

Heady made his first trip out of the United States in 1947 when he and William G. Murray attended the International Conference of Agricultural Economists in Devon, England. There he made contact with several agricultural economists from the developing countries. Additionally he had the opportunity to get better acquainted with several prominent U.S. agricultural economists, among them O. B. Jessness and Earl Butz. For the next decade Earl was heavily involved in research, writing, and teaching in the United States. This was the period during which he wrote *Economics of Agricultural Production and Resource Use* and, with H. R. Jensen, *Farm Management Economics* (Englewood Cliffs, N.J.: Prentice Hall, 1954). But the international dimension was not altogether absent from his thinking because he worked closely with several students from other countries, most notably Omar Wahby and Abdel El-Attar from Egypt, Husain from India, William Darcovich from Yugoslavia, Schalk du Toit from the Union of South Africa, and Ole Sanberg and Sigmund Borgan from the Scandinavian countries. Yujiro Hayami from Japan was also in Ames during the latter part of this period. All of these people remained friends and supporters of Heady and he had further contact with them in their own countries at sometime during his life.

In 1956 Earl was provided an opportunity to visit Japan. In 1958 he made the first of several trips to India to attend the Tenth International Conference of Agricultural Economists in Mysore. Supported by a grant from the Rockefeller Foundation, he returned to India in 1959 to advise the Ministry of Food and Agriculture. This time he spent six weeks within the country and returned concerned about the poverty he had witnessed and convinced that the United States and other countries had to do more to help the developing countries of the world. Consistent with his positive, optimistic attitude he did not look upon the situation as hopeless. Earl was convinced that with appropriate economic policies, people of India could enjoy a decent standard of living within half a century. He was impressed with the opportunities he saw everywhere for the productive application of economic analysis to the country's problems.

Upon his return to Ames following his second visit to India, Earl shared with me on several occasions his doubts about the importance of what he was doing on the domestic front. He remarked that making corn belt agriculture marginally more efficient hardly seemed important to him compared with the needs of India and the other developing countries. Although he continued to work on U.S. problems, he never escaped the conviction that the important economic problems of the world were to be found in the developing countries.

After 1959 Heady travelled to all parts of the world. In the fall of 1983, he told me he had crossed the Atlantic Ocean 125 times. Typically during the latter half of his active career he was out of the country four or five times per year, on occasion for periods of four to six weeks. His time in Ames came to be nothing more than interludes between his foreign and domestic trips.

Heady's foreign activities involved funded projects with (1) Nacional Agrarian University at Chapingo, Mexico, a project financed by the Ford Foundation; (2) Thailand; and (3) Indonesia. In each of the latter two countries the Ministry of Agriculture was the principal cooperating agency with funding provided by U.S.A.I.D. All three of these projects required that a party of ISU staff members and/or advanced students reside in the recipient country and that personnel from each country undertake advanced training in the United States, typically at ISU. The projects extended over several years and Thailand and Indonesia developed a sizeable cadre of professionals who had training in the United States, often with Heady. The Iowa State group in both Thailand and Indonesia welcomed Earl with open arms and treated him as a visiting dignitary. He enjoyed the interaction he had on these trips and was especially delighted to see former students making excellent professional progress in these complex environments. In later years he had a liaison with Ethiopia and spent time there.

During his later years Heady also visited many developed countries. In the early 1960s he was a U.S. representative to the Organization for European Economic Cooperation and Development (OEECD), which involved a number of trips to Europe and interaction with economists from the European Community countries. He visited the Scandinavian countries frequently because he had a number of close professional friends there who persistently urged him to come and made arrangements so that he could do so. He had a great deal of respect for the research being done in these countries. He felt that Sweden in particular was involved in imaginative and creative research in the agricultural sciences.

No account of Heady's international efforts would be complete without mention of his relationship with the Iron Curtain countries. Several Russian agricultural economists visited Ames during and after World War II. By 1961, Earl's work was known in Russia through the three major books he had by then published.[13] An acquaintance in Russia took the initiative in inviting Earl to visit. The initial trip in 1962 was supported by the National Science Foundation and provided for Earl to visit and lecture in Hungary and Poland as well as in Russia. On these trips, his hosts typically lined up a full schedule for Heady and made full use of his talents. The first trip behind the Iron Curtain was a memorable one for Heady. He emphasized again and again that the communist bloc countries had the same problems of resource allocation and income distribution as the capitalist countries and that the same tools were relevant for analyzing economic problems under both systems. Although he appreciated the lip service his colleagues in these countries had to pay to Marxist economies he insisted that they could not effectively analyze and improve their system until they became objective scientists.

The easy rapport he established with his hosts in all of these countries led to invitations to visit in their homes and frank discus-

sions on life behind the Iron Curtain. Heady was convinced the
people of these countries wanted much the same material amenities as
Americans and had the same concerns for and problems with their
youngsters as parents did in the United States. They were also concerned about freedom to live their own lives, to travel, to enjoy decent
housing, to receive competent medical care, and especially to prop-
erly educate their children. Upon his return from these visits Earl
spoke optimistically about the future of East-West relationships and
was confident that in fifty years the two economic systems would be
essentially the same. He strongly urged much more in the way of
exchanges and interaction between the East and the West.

Heady undertook to arrange a seminar between the two blocs on
methodology for agricultural economists. This conference met in
Keszthely, Hungary, from June 21 through July 1, 1968, with approximately two dozen participants divided more or less evenly from
East and West. Heady was elected the permanent president of this
group, and they planned a second meeting in Russia in 1974. With
Ford and Rockefeller Foundation support, Earl travelled frequently
to the Iron Curtain countries after 1968 until his retirement in 1983.
He served in a consulting capacity to research institutes, agricultural
ministries, and universities in Russia, Poland, Hungary, Rumania,
Yugoslavia, and Czechoslovakia. He also aided the foundations in
selecting staff members and students for study grants in the United
States.

In addition to the Iron Curtain countries, Heady was an invited
lecturer at universities and scientific academies in Germany, Egypt,
Nigeria, Turkey, India, Thailand, Japan, the Philippines, Canada,
Mexico, Argentina, Australia, Pakistan, Lebanon, Ethiopia, Ghana,
and Zaire. There were few countries of the world he had not visited
by 1983.

NOTES

1. Years before Earl came to Ames, Nourse left Iowa State to join the Brookings
Institute and later became the first Chairman of the Council of Economic Advisers
under President Harry Truman.

2. Among the group who were contemporaries at Iowa State in 1950 were
Emery Castle, Russell Olson, Howard Ottosen, John Hopkin, Harold Jensen, Earl

Swanson, R. J. Hildreth, Ernest Nisius, Gordon Ball, and Carroll Hess.

3. Earl O. Heady, "Elementary Models in Farm Production Economics Research," *Journal of Farm Economics* 30(May 1948): 201–225.

4. Heady attempted missionary work among his colleagues from the North Central Region in a farm management research workshop held July 18–31, 1948, at Deer Path Camp, Land O'Lakes, Wisconsin. The core of his presentations was material from the 1948 article on methodology. Professor Heady continued his efforts to win converts to his own perspective on farm management research methodology at a similar workshop held at Blackduck Lake in Minnesota during the summer of 1949.

5. Lee Day, "The Administration of Resources in Pork Production as Related to the Marginal Rates of Corn/Protein Substitution," Master of Science thesis, Iowa State University, 1946.

6. There were probably a dozen publications dealing with the production function in one way or another during the first decade. Heady's pattern of involving a graduate student intent upon developing a thesis was repeated many times following the initial example of Lee Day.

7. Notable among the group of ISU agricultural scientists with whom Earl collaborated were Damon Catron and Vaughan Speer from the Department of Animal Science and John Pesek from the Department of Agronomy.

8. Earl O. Heady, "The Economics of Rotations with Farm and Production Policy Applications," *Journal of Farm Economics* 30(1948): 645–664. The ideas in this article developed out of preliminary planning for a dissertation project by Harold Jensen entitled "Economics of Crop Rotations," Iowa State University, 1950.

9. Earl O. Heady, "Simplified Presentation and Logical Aspects of Linear Programming Techniques," Iowa State University Extension Bulletin 34, May 1954.

10. Clifford Hildreth and Steve Reiter, "On the Choice of a Crop Rotation Plan," in Tjalling C. Koopmans, ed., *Activity Analysis of Production and Allocation*, Chapter 11, Cowles Commission Monograph No. 13 (New York: Wiley, 1951).

Richard A. King, "Some Applications of Activity Analysis in Agricultural Economics," *Journal of Farm Economics* 35(1953): 823–833.

Earl Swanson and Kirk Fox, "The Selection of Livestock Enterprises by Activity Analysis," *Journal of Farm Economics*, 36(1954): 78–86.

11. Associate Director of the Agriculture Experiment Station at Iowa State at that time.

12. Sophisticated new software related to linear programming also invited researchers to order more output than they could handle. With the successors to the IBM 650 and parametric programming routines it became possible literally to generate stacks of output—more than the author had time to digest. The temptation arose again to substitute alternative assumptions concerning restraints, prices and coefficients for critical judgment.

13. Earl O. Heady, *Economics of Agricultural Production and Resource Use* (Englewood Cliffs, N.J.: Prentice Hall, 1952); Earl O. Heady and John Dillon, *Agricultural Production Functions* (Ames: Iowa State University Press, 1961); and Earl O. Heady and Wilfred Candler, *Linear Programming in Agriculture* (Ames: Iowa State University Press, 1958).

WILLIAM G. MURRAY

2 *Earl Heady*

Intellectual Breakthrough

The transition from Ted Schultz to Earl Heady at Iowa State University involved a long period with plenty of complications. It happened while I was head of the Department of Economics and Sociology from 1943 to 1955. Schultz resigned as head in 1942 to go to the University of Chicago. In those years the head of the department had a great deal of authority, especially in recruiting, salaries, and promotions. Back in 1940, Heady, who had a bachelor's and a master's degree from the University of Nebraska, applied to Schultz for an instructorship and an opportunity to work for his Ph.D. at Iowa State. Schultz was impressed with Heady's record and offered him the instructorship and the Ph.D. opportunity that he began in the fall of 1940.

When Schultz resigned in 1942 Heady was still an instructor working on his doctorate. When I took over as head I was faced not only with the vacancy created by Schultz's resignation but by a number of other vacancies as a result of a virtual exodus of agricultural economics staff who left soon after Schultz did.

Instead of replacing Schultz and the others who left, we got the deans to let us use the vacant salaried positions to bring in for periods

---

William G. Murray was Professor Emeritus, Department of Economics, Iowa State University.

of one to six months the prospects we wanted to consider. The prospects were given assignments in short-term teaching and research that gave them an opportunity to get acquainted with us and we with them. But we didn't get any prospect that in our opinion matched the candidate we wanted to fill Schultz's shoes.

During this period we began to realize that we had on the staff a young instructor by the name of Earl Heady who had a great deal of potential. As it happened, I was his major professor on his Ph.D. committee, so I had an excellent opportunity to size him up. I became thoroughly convinced in 1945, when Heady received his doctor's degree, that he had what we had been looking for in a replacement for Schultz.

I had my feeling confirmed one day by Margaret Reid, who was leaving to join Schultz at the University of Chicago. She stopped me in the hall—I can remember it as if it was yesterday—to tell me that Heady was the man we were looking for to replace Schultz. Of course this was not an identical replacement. The two were entirely different, but they were both intellectual leaders in their own way.

In the fall of 1947, Earl Heady challenged the current conventional theory of farm production economics at the Seventh Conference of the International Association of Agricultural Economists held at Darlington, England. Earl and I represented Iowa State at the conference. Earl at this time was beginning to formulate the ideas that in 1952 would form the basis of his major book.

It was a fascinating experience to watch this young thirty-one-year-old farm economist present his new challenging ideas to a group that included many of the outstanding farm economists in the world. I remember well how many of the leaders were baffled and upset by Heady's new concepts, which included statistical and mathematical elements they found difficult to understand. There was a definite chill in the air as the majority had some of their cherished ideas challenged by this young man from the United States they had never heard of before. In the years that followed, this confrontation happened again and again but with more and more converts accepting Heady's new ideas.

Kenneth Galbraith of Harvard reviewed Heady's first major manuscript, *Economics of Agricultural Production and Resource Use,* for

Prentice Hall and wrote to Heady, "I think this is really a masterpiece, both of technique and of exposition, and I do not know how to congratulate you adequately on the achievement." This book, published in 1952, established Heady's reputation.

How can one explain Heady's rise to the top? At least part was the interdisciplinary combination of Kenneth Boulding's creativity, John Nordin's emphasis on economic theory, Gerhard Tintner's and Leo Hurwicz's solid exposition of econometrics, and George Snedecor's applications of statistical methods to agricultural problems. There were others, of course, but these were a closely knit group of colleagues who served first as his teachers in his Ph.D. program and later as individuals he could consult with and ask to evaluate his ideas.

This unusual group of outstanding theorists in related fields gave Heady a marvelous opportunity to develop his theories and to test them. Gerhard Tinter, who had his office in the same building with Heady, was actually a member of three departments—Economics, Statistics, and Mathematics. Kenneth Boulding, also housed in the same building as Heady, was considered an economist but he never let that designation keep him from delving into other social sciences. As an agricultural economist, Heady worked in an unusually stimulating environment. But we must not overlook the fact that Heady himself had the ability to take advantage of this extraordinary intellectual climate.

Heady had many attractive offers to go to prestigious universities. (I remember the head of a department from a major university who rented a room in an Ames hotel for about a week determined that in this period he could get Earl Heady to come to his institution.) When he requested them, he was granted leaves of absence to accept short-term appointments at other universities who were interested in having him on a permanent basis. He served as a visiting professor at the University of Illinois, North Carolina State University, the University of California, and Harvard University.

I spent much of my time until I gave up the headship of the department urging Heady to turn down offers from other institutions. With the help of the deans and the president we were able to accelerate Heady's promotion in rank and salary so that the instructor in

1945 with a nine-month salary of $2,750 was a full professor in 1949 with a twelve-month salary of $6,000, which was raised to $8,200 in 1950 and to $10,000 in 1952. (His salary in 1952 was higher than mine on my recommendation.)

Most of the time Earl's increases in salary came in connection with an outside offer. Since there were numerous offers, Heady received numerous salary increases. Fortunately, however, in 1951 there was opportunity to grant Earl an increase without an outside offer. After Earl received this increase he sent the deans and me a letter, a portion of which read:

> I wish to express my appreciation for the recent salary increase. Not so much for the money itself but more because of the expression behind it. It has boosted my morale more than anything else that has ever happened to me at Iowa State. The increase has given me the feeling that Iowa State is both acquainted with and interested in my efforts as much as outsiders. I appreciate your expression and will do my utmost to justify your expressed faith in my work.

There was definitely something at Iowa State that was sufficiently attractive to cause him to turn down the numerous generous offers he received. Iowa State's attraction for Heady was made up of a least three factors. The first we have already described—the interdisciplinary intellectual environment. This provided him with the knowledge and stimulus he found so helpful in his creative writing.

A second factor, which may have been even more important in his decision to remain at Iowa State, was what I called his "pipe line." He and his graduate students had a tremendous research program in operation that involved collecting an amazing amount of data. This data entered the pipe line and then went through various stages of classification and analysis. Eventually it came out the other end of the pipe line in the form of articles, books, and Ph.D. theses. If Heady had accepted one of the tempting offers that came his way it is unlikely he would have been able to establish as successful a pipe line in his new position, at least not for several years. To this must be added the fact that in his agricultural training in Nebraska as well as at Iowa State, Heady had developed excellent working relationships with other agricultural scientists, including agronomists and animal scientists. The result of this cooperation was a large number of agricultural publications based on Corn Belt farm data.

A third factor that helps to explain Heady's desire to stay at Iowa State was the supporting attitude of his faculty friends and university administrators, and the advantages of living in Ames, which among other things provided excellent schools for the Heady children.

29- 51

ROLAND K. ROBERTS

DARYLL E. RAY

DONALD O. MITCHELL

RAYMOND JOE SCHATZER

3

Agricultural Sector Simulation Modeling

A gricultural sector simulation modeling has taken an increasingly important role in agricultural economics research and policy-making in the last three decades and especially in the last fifteen years as computer capacity has improved and research concerns have shifted toward dynamic problems of U.S. agriculture. Earl Heady's flexibility, foresight and ability to adjust to changes in research technology and the demands of emerging issues was typified when he recognized the value of simulation modeling as a problem-solving method and added it to his collection of research tools.

Roland K. Roberts and Daryll E. Ray are Professors, Department of Agricultural Economics and Rural Sociology, University of Tennessee. Donald O. Mitchell is Senior Economist, International Economics Department, World Bank. Raymond Joe Schatzer is Associate Professor, Department of Agricultural Economics, Oklahoma State University.

Although Heady was not at the forefront of efforts to develop simulation modeling techniques, his contributions to agricultural sector simulation modeling have been significant. His most significant contribution was the first multiple-commodity policy simulation model to generate both aggregate and individual commodity results. His was also the first simulation modeling effort to disaggregate input demands by commodity and link those demands to commodity production.

SIMULATION MODELS DEFINED

A simulation model as defined in this chapter is a mathematical model representing the key elements of a real world process or phenomenon. Thus, a simulation model can represent an economy, a decision process, a biological process or almost anything that can be quantitatively described. Simulation models of an economy or sector typically have two distinctive features that separate them from regression equations. First, they are dynamic in that the results from one time period become inputs into subsequent time periods. Second, they have linkages among equations in such a way as to create an interdependent system. The purpose of constructing a model is to allow experiments or simulations to be performed on the model from which inferences can be drawn about the real world system.

Two main types of simulation models appear in the agricultural economics literature: econometric models and systems models. Econometric simulation models consist of econometrically estimated multiequation models of an economy or sector. Tinbergen (1939) is generally regarded as the father of econometric modeling based on his work on business cycles. This work was expanded and refined by Haavelmo (1944), Koopmans (1950), Klein (1950) and many others. The second type of simulation model, the systems simulation approach, involves the mathematical representation of an economy where the model is not necessarily based on estimated relationships or even on historical information. The systems simulation technique is less structured and more flexible than econometric modeling techniques. Forrester (1961) is generally credited with the initial work in this field.

Simulation models are used primarily for forecasting, for impact analysis and for improved understanding of the real world. The advantage of simulation models is their ability to determine the quantitative importance of system interactions. Simulation models make it possible to determine the consequences of changes in one component of a model on other components. This can include evaluating the consequences of changing levels of an exogenous variable on the projected value of an endogenous variable or evaluating a policy change on a target variable such as income distribution. This may alert an analyst or policymaker to unexpected linkages in the system. Another strength of simulation models is that the lack of rigid structure allows the model to be focused on the topic of particular interest while ignoring or giving less complete treatment to other aspects of the overall sector. Unfortunately, this is also a major weakness of simulation models because the full extent of system interrelationships may not be understood. This can lead to problems when a critical aspect of a system is not adequately modeled.

Simulation models can be solved as either stochastic or deterministic processes depending on whether variables are assumed to have probability distributions. With a deterministic solution, a single value is obtained from each equation and a single solution exists for the model variables. A stochastic simulation is obtained when some or all of the model variables are allowed to take different values for the same period. For example, crop yields are subject to variability due to weather. This can be captured in a stochastic simulation by allowing yields to vary according to a probability distribution. The model is then simulated many times to obtain an average result around which confidence limits can be placed. This type of simulation is often called Monte Carlo simulation.

DEVELOPMENT OF SIMULATION MODELS IN AGRICULTURAL ECONOMICS

The development of simulation models in agricultural economics has been driven by changing problems that required new methods of analysis. During the 1920s and 1930s, research in agricultural economics was designed to help farmers improve their management skills by reducing costs and increasing efficiency. Accounting and budgeting techniques were the first tools of farm management and production economics. By the 1940s and 1950s, linear programming techniques began to be used for resource allocation and least-cost applications at the firm level. This greatly increased the analytic capability of agricultural economists to study profit maximization, optimal investment decisions and adjustments to changes in market conditions. The emergence of computer capabilities and the strong interest in problems of farm firm management led to an explosion of modeling activity.

The 1960s saw increased interest in a more complete understanding of aggregate supply behavior for use in formulating and analyzing policy. This was brought on by growing surpluses. Research required improved understanding of how groups of farmers were likely to respond to various economic and policy incentives. Initial efforts to understand such group responses were directed at extending existing research tools. The general approach was to define a series of representative farm firms and use linear programming on each with various combinations of commodity prices to obtain synthetic supply response functions. These were then weighted by numbers of firms in each category to build up aggregate supply response functions for each commodity. A major difficulty with these studies was the enormous amount of resources required to build and run such models. Another was the difficulty of obtaining credible estimates due to aggregation problems.

Modeling projects typically included efforts to assess the magnitudes and incidence of government program costs and benefits under different program alternatives. Much of the effort was based on existing program structure rather than on a broader range of alternative solutions. To some extent, this reflected the limitations of scope and breadth in the technology of analysis. Because this analysis was largely done with programming models, it was very difficult to capture the dynamic aspects of farm programs over time. In their book *Future Farm Programs,* Heady et al. (1972) began to bridge the gap between programming models and simulation models. Resource use in agriculture was examined using an aggregate simulation model, while land retirement schemes were examined with programming models.

Econometric analysis was widely used to better understand farm response, demand and resource requirements during the 1940s, 1950s and 1960s; however simulation models did not evolve until later. Heady was one of the first agricultural economists to apply regression techniques to agriculture. In 1946, he empirically estimated the first production function for agricultural firms using cross-sectional data from Iowa farms (Heady, 1946). The book *Agricultural Production Functions* by Heady and Dillon (1961) culminated much of this work and became a classic in agricultural economics.

Econometric equations were linked together to form the first econometric models to analyze market interactions and market dynamics. These techniques were applied to agricultural economics beginning in the late 1950s. The first subsector simulation model applied to agriculture appears to be a four equation model of the feed-livestock economy by Foote (1953). The first sector simulation model appears to be by Cromarty (1959). This model was developed as a sector model to link with models of the U.S. economy being developed by Klein (1950) and Klein and Goldberger (1955). Among the earliest application of these models by Heady and his students were Heady and Tweeten (1963), Scott and Heady (1966), and Shechter (1968). These models were used to analyze problems that could not easily be considered with programming models or budgeting techniques. For example, Shechter used a stochastic simulation model to derive empirical decision rules for operating a U.S. feed grain program under yield uncertainty. Scott and Heady considered the regional demand for farm machinery.

The earliest examples of Monte Carlo simulation were applications to complex production systems under uncertainty such as milk procurement policies for cheese plants (Glickstein et al., 1962) and management policies under price and weather uncertainties for a large California range-feedlot operation (Halter and Dean, 1965). The first applications of systems simulation were the development of models of Venezuela by Holland et al. (1966) and of Nigeria by Manetsch et al. (1971). The Nigerian project model was directed by Glenn Johnson and consisted of a multidisciplinary group of primarily systems scientists and agricultural economists working during the 1965–1971 period.

The events of the early 1970s saw a major shift in focus in

agricultural economics research away from domestic resource use and toward macroeconomic and trade issues. Prior to the 1970s, agricultural prices were relatively stable and the primary issues facing the profession involved resource use, efficiency and government programs to control supply at a minimum cost. Demand was stable from year to year because it depended primarily upon U.S. domestic demand, which changed slowly over time. The export market was viewed as a dumping ground for surpluses, not a commercial outlet for production. In that type of environment, little uncertainty existed and economists searched for optimizing solutions to resource allocation problems. The primary question was how to produce, not how much to produce. Perhaps the first consequence of the changing focus away from domestic resource use to international markets was the realization that the levels of prices and the demands on U.S. production capabilities were large unknowns.

The focus of farm policy shifted away from supply control and price supports during the 1970s. There was less concern about the general public costs of traditional farm programs and the income transfer to the farm sector. The impact of nonfarm programs on the farm firm and the food and fiber sector became a major area of interest. Environment, work safety, and resource use and availability became focal points for both farm firm and broader policy analysis. New analytical tools and new data sources were often required. Farm adjustment models were modified to become water assessment models funded by the Environmental Protection Agency or energy models funded by the Department of Energy. In analytical terms, there was much more concern with trying to capture firm-production system interactions and farm-sector interactions.

The increased market uncertainty during the 1970s caused farmers and agribusiness firms to focus on market intelligence and not just on resource allocation problems. This created a demand for better marketing information. Programming models which had been the staple of the 1960s were not well suited to providing short-term forecasts of prices and export level, and simulation models began to emerge.

The work of Ray (1971) and Ray and Heady (1972, 1974) was the first large sector simulation model of U.S. agriculture with detailed commodity submodels. This model included agricultural inputs and outputs by commodity and was used to evaluate various government policies for wheat, feed grains, soybeans, cotton, tobacco and livestock. It became the basis for additional policy analysis by CARD during the 1970's and early 1980s using simulation models (Reynolds et al., 1975; Heady et al., 1977; Roberts, 1979; Roberts and Heady, 1980; English et al., 1981; Schatzer et al., 1981; Christensen and Heady, 1983; Drabenstott, 1981).

Following the early work on sector simulation models in the 1970s a virtual explosion of modeling activities occurred in nearly all areas of agricultural economics. By 1977, a U.S. General Accounting Office report (1977) identified fifty simulation models of policy analysis in agriculture. Thompson (1981), in a review of models of international agricultural trade, documented a large number of models and nearly three hundred citations on this topic.

The adoption of simulation models for policy work can be traced through the U.S. Department of Agriculture from the early 1970s. Prior to that, modeling work for policy analysis began in the Economic Research Service (ERS) during the mid 1960s with the development of the ERS National Model in conjunction with CARD at Iowa State University. This large linear programming model and smaller regional models developed under the direction of the regional research committees were the mainstay of policy analysis in the 1960s. Heady played a dominant role in this work. Recursive programming was introduced into these models in the late 1960s to try to improve their use for forecasting accuracy.

The Forecast Support Group of ERS was one of the first groups to use econometric simulation models. Econometrically estimated commodity supply and demand relationships became generally available in the 1950s and 1960s but were not used for routine ongoing commodity price forecasts or policy analysis. During the 1970s, the Forecast Support Group of ERS was one of the first groups to systematically use commodity models for generating short-term forecasts and longer-term projections.

POLYSIM (Ray, 1973) was the first agricultural sector simulation model used extensively by ERS for policy analysis. While not an econometric model, it included a commodity structure similar to the model developed by Ray (1971) at Iowa State University. The POLYSIM analysis approach used elasticities and percentage changes from an established baseline set of data to estimate impacts of commodity program modifications. This produced a model that could evaluate policy changes quickly and inexpensively. The POLYSIM model was used extensively for analysis of the 1973 and 1977 farm bills.

In the early 1970s commercial forecasting groups began to develop econometric models. The major groups were Chase Econometric, Data Resources, Inc., and Wharton Econometrics. The first models became available in about 1975 and both the Economic Research Service and the Congressional Budget Office subscribed to these services and used the models for policy analysis.

SIMULATION MODELING'S CONTRIBUTION AND IMPACT ON THE AGRICULTURAL ECONOMICS PROFESSION

Perhaps the greatest contribution of simulation modeling has been enhanced appreciation of the interrelationships among commodities within the agricultural sector. Use of agricultural sector simulation models allowed the measurement of secondary effects from policy changes and other economic outcomes. This increased knowledge of cross-commodity effects has had a major influence on policy discussions because policy actions being considered by one commodity group could no longer be considered in isolation from other groups. This has opened policy discussions to a broader set of constituents, including consumers and producers of foreign countries.

Sector simulation models also have allowed consideration of year-to-year dynamics of sector responses. For policy analysis this is often more important than static equilibrium comparisons because much of policy analysis is done in a rolling environment. The full consequences of a particular policy are seldom complete before a new policy is introduced which sets forth a new set of dynamics. Static equilibrium analysis is not well suited to such comparisons, while sector simulation models are.

Nevertheless, some researchers have argued that simulation models have not lived up to their expectations. Just and Rausser (1981) have argued that agricultural simulation models have not performed very well for forecasting purposes. Johnson (1981) has argued that they have not had a significant impact on policy decisions.

Thompson (1981), on the other hand, has credited agricultural sector simulation models with transforming the policy process into a battleground, with every constituent group using a simulation model to support its position.

The perception that models have not lived up to their billings seems to have emerged from the increasingly complex problems facing agriculture. National and international policies regarding macroeconomics, trade policies and agriculture have become increasingly interrelated, and with these changes have come greater price and export variability. This has forced agricultural policy to deal increasingly with nonagricultural sectors in designing agricultural policies. The more widespread availability of simulation models has also highlighted the conflict between different agricultural sectors and brought more commodity groups into the discussions.

HEADY'S CONTRIBUTION TO SIMULATION MODELING

Heady's contributions to agricultural sector simulation modeling were significant. These contributions are outlined in greater detail here, giving insight into those factors that motivated his thrust in this area.

The research project that generated the original econometric agricultural policy simulation model at CARD (Ray, 1971) was inspired by Heady's desire to econometrically model agricultural resource markets. In 1963, Heady and Tweeten (1963) published the first attempt at specifying and empirically estimating aggregate demand relationships for each of the major agricultural resource categories. Using their book as a touchstone, Heady and his students produced a series of resource demand studies that provided additional detail and investigated regional demand differences. Studies by Helmers (1965) on farm labor, Minden (1965) on machinery, Scott (1965) on farm buildings and Lin (1967) on aggregate factor demand were part of this series. Heady and Ray began discussions that would eventually add to this body of knowledge.

The simulation models of aggregate agriculture by Lin (1967) and by Tyner and Tweeten (1968) had a particularly strong impression on the design of the first CARD simulation model. The Tyner and Tweeten model included a well-developed U.S. aggregate input demand section with separate relationships for the major factors of agricultural production. In the simulation process, an aggregate Cobb-Douglas production function was used to estimate supply with coefficients estimated from factor shares and input quantities fed from the estimated input demand equations. Aggregate relationships for quantity demand, price, income and expenses were included to complete the model (Tyner, 1966; Tyner and Tweeten, 1965, 1968).

Since these models were highly aggregated, analysis of commodity policy was largely precluded. Ray and Heady discussed developing commodity submodels for the major crop categories. Each submodel would include an input demand section in addition to supply and demand relationships. From the standpoint of the resource markets, input demands would be investigated by commodity rather than by other delineations such as geographical regions. The submodels would be designed so the influence of commodity program instruments could be isolated and then varied during the simulation phase of the research. Heady was enthusiastic about the project and suggested adding a livestock sector and a set of aggregation relationships to fully encompass U.S. agriculture. These additions would eventually improve the analytical capabilities of the model as well as improve communication of results by allowing values for net farm income and other highly watched aggregate variables to be reported.

While the model was being developed, Heady and Ray discussed the policy alternatives that should be simulated. Their primary interest was to simulate what the impact on agriculture would have been if other farm policy regimes had been used for all or a portion of the historical estimation period. In addition to the deterministic historical simulations, Heady was extremely interested in using the model for projecting into the future for increased policy analysis flexibility.

Heady was characteristically very supportive during model development, but he went beyond that. He said this project was generating a significant modeling initiative that would produce the profession's first aggregate econometric farm policy model with detailed commodity submodels.

Overview of the Model

The commodity submodels in order of their appearance in the model were livestock, feed grains, wheat, soybeans, cotton and tobacco. The relationships in each submodel sequentially depicted the commodity's yearly production cycle from acreage planted (in the crop models) to the level of resource use, to production, to price, to commodity disposition, and finally to gross income. The submodels, or blocks of equations, were brought together to form the overall simulation model as a representation of the sequential and recursive nature of agricultural production.

The submodel organization permitted the explicit inclusion of appropriate government policy variables for individual commodities. Primary and secondary effects of a change in commodity policy variables were traceable through the equations of the relevant commodity, related commodities and total agriculture. The relationships in each submodel were grouped into pre-input and output sections. These broad groups were also used by Tyner and Tweeten (1968) in their aggregate model of agriculture. In addition, the simulator contained a set of identities which summed variable estimates for the separate commodities into national estimates.

DATA. Time series data for many of the commodity resource demand variables were not published and had to be developed from cost and return studies, input-output studies and published and unpublished data from the U.S. Department of Agriculture (Ray, 1971).

ECONOMETRIC CONSIDERATIONS. The recursive structure of the model simplified the simulation procedure and under certain conditions allowed the use of ordinary least squares to estimate the relationships. Two-stage least squares also was used to estimate equations with more than one endogenous variable allowing for a generalized variance-covariance matrix. Fuller and Martin's (1961, 1962) autoregressive least squares procedure was applied to equations with one endogenous variable. Autoregressive two stage least squares was applied to equations with more than one endogenous variable. Generally, the coefficient estimates of the autoregression techniques were used in the simulation model if the autocorrelation coefficient was significantly different from zero. All relationships were estimated using annual time series data for 1930–1967. Estimated relationships were presented in Ray and Heady 1972 and 1974 and discussed in Ray 1971.

THE SIMULATION PROCESS. Since the simulation model was recursive, the computer program solved each equation sequentially. When each of the equations for each of the submodels was solved, one time period for the agricultural sector was described and the computer returned to the first equation to begin generating information for the next period. In this and remaining periods, variable levels were included that were estimated in previous periods.

RESULTS. The estimated model was simulated with no changes in parameter estimates or exogenous data to test the model's ability to predict actual variable levels of the agricultural sector between 1932 and 1967. On the basis of computed Theil (1958) coefficients and scatter diagrams, the model was concluded to simulate historical data with sufficient accuracy to permit using the model to conduct simulation experiments.

Simulation experiments included (a) the removals of government price and income support programs, (b) increases in input prices, (c) restrictions on production elasticities, (d) variations in commodity support prices, and (e) limitations on acreages.

Free Market. Farm prices and incomes declined substantially in the absence of government programs. Results indicated that without government price and income support programs, farmers would have had less incentive and financial resources to purchase labor-saving capital inputs. This implication must have been surprising to individuals who advocated those programs to save the family farm.

Input Prices and Technology Held Constant. Simulations looking at the effects of increased input prices and slowed technological advance indicated that reduced production and lower input expenditures caused average annual net farm income during this time to increase by about one-quarter. If the farm technology of the 1932–1939 period (as represented by the parameters of crop production functions) remained in effect through 1987, net farm income would have increased by one-fifth during the 1959–1967 period when only technology was held constant and by one-third when input prices were held fixed at 1932–1939 levels as well.

Changed Price Support Levels. The sensitivity of resource-use levels, commodity prices and incomes to changes in crop price support levels was investigated by assuming that support prices for each of the model crops were increased by 10 percent in the analysis and decreased by 10 percent. The results suggested that the intended price and income benefits of raising price support levels were partially dissipated without added acreage or other supply controls. The increased production in response to higher support prices exerted downward pressure on market prices which partially offset the price raising effects of higher support prices.

Policies to Sharply Curtail Acreage. Perhaps the most striking result of simulations looking at sharply curtailing wheat and feed grain acreage was that government policies which increased farm prices and income did not "hold" labor in farming but rather encouraged the substitution of highly productive capital inputs for labor. The rate at which resource adjustments occur at the micro-level in agriculture were influenced to an important extent by the ability of individual farmers to finance the use of capital inputs and the prospect of being able to do so in the future.

A STEPPING STONE AND A CHALLENGE. The concluding remarks section of Ray and Heady (1972) summarized the need for agricultural models as perceived in the early 1970s and suggested that this model might be a stepping stone to modeling efforts in the future.

> Ideally, a policy simulation model of the agricultural industry should serve as an econometric map of the agricultural economy within the framework of the total national economy. The interactions of the commodity and resource markets within the agricultural sector should be represented, as should the lines of influence between the agricultural sector and the national economy. The structural relationships should incorporate government policy variables in sufficient detail that a broad range of economic policies can be simulated. The model should be capable of analyzing not only the effects of an agricultural policy change on the area of its immediate application but also the effects on related agricultural commodities, the entire agricultural sector, and the econ-

omy as a whole. Research is needed to develop a definitive model of the agricultural sector that can be tied into existing national forecasting models. Much of the data and all of the expertise already exists. Although the model developed in this study is most suited for historical simulations, it is hoped that it might serve as a stepping stone to the construction of a comprehensive forecasting model of the agricultural industry.

First Major Revision of the Model

With Heady's encouragement and at the request of the Office of Planning and Evaluation, Office of the Secretary of Agriculture, U.S. Department of Agriculture, the simulation model developed by Ray (1971) was extended and adapted to provide long-run projections and insights into the consequences of alternative future export levels, government agricultural policies and levels of production efficiency (Reynolds et al., 1975).

The framework of the initial CARD simulation model was broadly restructured. The model still depicted the sequential nature of the agricultural production cycle from one year to the next by using pre-input, input and output sections for each endogenous commodity. The pre-input section was essentially the same as Ray's (1971), except the acreage equations were reestimated. In the input section, the fertilizer, labor and miscellaneous expenses equations were reestimated on a per acre basis. The output sections were completely restructured. Production was estimated using an exogenously projected yield per acre rather than the Cobb-Douglas production functions used by Ray. Domestic demand was divided into separate equations for seed, food and feed.

ANALYSIS OF FUTURE ALTERNATIVES. Seven simulations were used to examine the future of American agriculture under alternative export levels, government agricultural policies and levels of production efficiency (Reynolds et al., 1975). The simulations were divided into two sets. The first set, trend future, examined the continuation of a government support program equivalent to the Agriculture and Consumer Protection Act of 1973 under the assumption of a continuation of historical trends in farm size, technology, resource use and export demands. The second set, maximum efficiency future, examined policies designed to increase total output and the efficiency of agriculture to meet an expanded world market.

Results indicated that the direction agricultural policy should take depended upon future export levels. The policy adopted would have long-run impacts on agriculture and the rest of society. If exports grew at trend projections, then government support policies would be needed. If the maximum efficiency future were obtained, then export supply capacity would be large. If exports expanded more than 50 percent above trend projections and the maximum efficiency future were obtained, then export supply capacity would be large. If exports expanded more than 50 percent above trend projections and the maximum efficiency were realized, then both consumers and the farm sector would gain from the productivity increases. At lower export levels, the increased efficiencies would worsen the problem of excess capacity.

TAX POLICY ANALYSIS. The revised model was also used by Heady et al. (1977) to analyze the effects on U.S. agriculture of three tax policies that might be used to restrain production and improve prices and incomes. The tax policies examined included a 20 percent tax on farm inputs, a 20 percent commodity tax on selected crops, and a 10 percent tax-in-kind on selected crops.

Results of the tax on farm inputs indicated that the inputs to be taxed must be carefully selected. Input use must be highly responsive to changes in input prices and must significantly affect crop prices through yield reductions. If tax revenues were returned to farmers, net farm income would rise by more than 10 percent above the free market alternative.

A 20 percent tax on wheat, feed grains, soybeans and cotton resulted in even higher tax revenues, with only a slight decrease in net farm income from the free market situation. If tax revenues were returned to farmers, net farm income would increase 22 percent.

The 10 percent tax-in-kind would be equivalent to the farmer serving as a tenant and paying 10 percent share rent to the government. If the government's share were used for food aid to countries unable to purchase food in the world market, then the tax-in-kind would raise net farm income by more than the other two alternatives considered. In addition, government-owned commodities could be used for food aid, buffer stocks or placed back on the domestic market. The current production, end-of-year inventories, civilian consumption, retail prices, farm-retail margins, gross farm value, cash receipts, and civilian consumption were determined by identities while the other five equations were estimated econometrically.

AGRICULTURAL POLICY IMPACTS ON THE LIVESTOCK SUBSECTOR. Selected agricultural policy impacts on the livestock subsector were analyzed using the revised model. Roberts and Heady (1980) considered two groups of policy alternatives: (1) supporting crop prices at parity levels and (2) increasing beef imports above trend levels. Eight simulations were developed to analyze several alternatives for the two policies. Results from the parity simulations showed that production of livestock and poultry commodities would decline, but prices received by farmers would increase sufficiently to increase cash receipts from livestock and poultry sales. Also, retail prices to consumers would increase sharply if crop prices were supported at parity levels. Results from the beef import simulations indicated the larger the increase in beef imports, the larger the decrease in retail prices of beef. On the other hand, farm prices to livestock, poultry and crop producers decreased, reducing farm-sector cash receipts.

Revision of the Input and Pre-Input Sections

The equations in the pre-input and input sections were reestimated with a similar structure to Ray (1971) using data for 1949 through 1976 (Schatzer et al., 1981b). Since the years included in the data series changed, the variables used to estimate particular equations changed. Also new variables to represent changes in government programs were added to the series.

These revised pre-input and input sections were then linked with the revised output sections estimated by Roberts and Heady (1979, 1980) to provide a complete simulation model of the U.S. agricultural sector. The revised model was used in several studies over the next few years. For each analysis, small changes in the model were introduced to better handle the alternatives to be considered. Also, reestimation with compatible real price variables occurred.

FARM SIZE AND YIELD PRODUCTIVITY IMPACTS. Heady was interested in using the updated and revised simulation model to extend earlier work on changes in farm structure, productivity and exports (Reynolds et al., 1975) by analyzing the dramatic changes that had occurred during the 1970s. Consequently, Schatzer et al. (1981a and 1983) and Roberts et al. (1980) analyzed the impacts of an expansion in farm size as measured by acres-per-farm and of increased yield productivity resulting from increased government expenditures on research and extension. Two farm-size trends and four yield productivity trends were analyzed. Export requirements to maintain prices at base scenario levels were also examined. Combinations of these assumed trend futures and price maintenance alternatives resulted in thirteen scenarios.

Results suggested that the direction U.S. farming should take depended upon the goals of U.S. society. If the goal was to increase net farm income, the United States should pursue a policy of not increasing real government expenditures on research and extension. If the goal was to increase net farm income per farm, then the United States should also try to increase the rate of growth in farm size. However, if the goal were simply to increase the size of total farm income and not per-farm income, then a continuation of the growth in farm size along historical productivity trends would be better. On the other hand, if the societal goal were to provide cheap food to consumers, then a path of increasing the real rate of government expenditures on agricultural-related research and extension and increasing the rate of growth in farm size should be followed. The results suggested this policy would devastate U.S. farmers unless additional government payments or increases in export demand for agricultural products above trend levels were forthcoming.

IMPACTS OF THE RUSSIAN GRAIN EMBARGO. The simulation model was used to analyze the potential long- term impacts on the U.S. agricultural sector created by the Russian grain embargo announced on January 4, 1980 (English et al., 1981). Four potential scenarios of the impact on U.S. grain exports were analyzed. These scenarios considered changes in the trend level of exports.

The analysis showed that the long-run change in the U.S. agricultural sector as a result of the embargo depended upon what happened to export trends. If efforts to replace Russian markets with markets in other countries were successful, only slight long-run impacts on the agricultural sector would be seen. On the other hand, if exports fell by the amount of the embargo and never recovered, prices of grains fell, inventories of grains increased and national net farm income decreased by over 25 percent from the base level by the year 2000. These results indicated that greater government presence would be required in the agricultural sector. Under all alternatives, the winner was probably the American consumer because of increased livestock production caused by the depressed crop sector.

ALTERNATIVE ENERGY ENVIRONMENTS. With the increase in energy prices in the late 1970s and early 1980s, Heady and his students became concerned about the influence a continual rise in energy prices would have on the structure of agriculture. Christensen et al. (1981a), Christensen et al. (1981b) and Christensen and Heady (1983) analyzed the impacts of alternative energy price scenarios on the long-run future of U.S. agriculture. Alternative energy price scenarios were chosen to include the range of gasoline price projections to the year 2000 found in a literature search. The objective was not to project energy prices but to examine possible impacts of alternative energy prices on agriculture. Five scenarios were developed to represent the range of projected energy prices. Two alternative trends in export levels were also considered.

As the level of energy prices increased, prices of energy intensive inputs such as fuel, fertilizer and pesticides increased, resulting in a decline in their purchases. Irrigation decreased significantly as energy prices increased. Machinery purchases declined as machinery was used less intensively.

Decreases in the use of fertilizer and pesticides led to a slower growth in crop yields. While the slowdown was not drastic, it did lead to decreased crop production and higher farm prices. Crop acreage increased as the energy price level increased but not enough to offset yield reductions caused by lower input usage. As crop prices increased, livestock producers faced rising feed costs. With higher feed costs, livestock production was reduced and farm prices for livestock increased. Retail meat prices also rose, leading consumers to reduce meat consumption slightly. National net farm income in the long-run actually increased as petroleum prices rose.

If petroleum prices were to rise worldwide and cause foreign real incomes to decline, U.S. exports of crop commodities might decrease. Lower export demand decreased the severity of the effects caused by rising petroleum prices.

Results suggested that *lack* of a specific long-run policy to stem the rise in petroleum prices would benefit farmers because average national farm income would increase.

Capital Demands for Alternative Economic and Policy Environments

Drabenstott (1981) added a finance sector to the simulation model to project capital flow demands and credit requirements of the U.S. agricultural finance sector. He reestimated the land price equations and machinery purchase equations and added equations for the financial assets held by the farm sector. He also disaggregated the value of land and buildings into the value of land and the value of buildings and land improvements. Nine scenarios were developed to analyze the impacts on the U.S. agricultural finance sector of alternative levels of crop exports, crop price supports, energy price trends, savings ratios, rates of inflation and restrictive ceilings on the level of agricultural lending.

Results from this analysis suggested that future capital flow would be sensitive to export levels, price support levels, energy prices and monetary conditions. Results also suggested that the U.S. agricultural sector would become much more highly leveraged in the future, implying that agriculture would feel the effects of business cycles and monetary policy much more acutely than in the past. The study also suggested that the farm sector would suffer greatly as national interest rates increased. While not able to predict the number of farmers who would fail, analysis of the results pointed toward farm failures. The results also suggested that in the future the supply of credit would play a much more dominant role in the farm sector.

The motivation behind Heady's desire to adapt the model for long-run projection was stated by him some years later at a symposium sponsored by the Federal Reserve Bank of Kansas City in 1981 (Heady, p. 136):

We have long used and extended an econometric, recursive simulation model. It has not emphasized short-run commodity price forecasts but has major focus on estimating, at the national level, the longer-run effects of changes in policies, market conditions, technological change, factor prices, and similar variables and farm structure generally—including numbers and sizes of farms, resource demand and input use, farm income, capital use and farm expenses, and similar variables. . . . The model is structured on an annual sequential basis since we are interested in tracing out the impact of such changes over a fairly extensive time period such as 10 or 20 years.

REFERENCES

Christensen, Douglas A., and Earl O. Heady. 1983. "The U.S. Agricultural Input Sector: How Will It Be Affected by Rising Energy Prices?" *North Central Journal of Agricultural Economics*, 5:83–96.

Christensen, Douglas A., R. Joe Schatzer, and Earl O. Heady. 1981a. "An Econometric Evaluation of Rising Petroleum Prices in Agriculture." In *Advances in Energy Technology*, papers presented at Eight Annual UMR-DNR Conferences on Energy, University of Missouri, Rolla, pp. 281–290.

Christensen, Douglas A., R. Joe Schatzer, Earl O. Heady, and Burton C. English. 1981b. *The Effects of Increased Energy Prices on U.S. Agriculture: An Econometric Approach*. CARD Report 104, Ames, Iowa: Center for Agricultural and Rural Development.

Cromarty, William A. 1959. "An Econometric Model for United States Agriculture." *American Statistical Association Journal*, 54:556–574.

Drabenstott, Mark R. 1981. "Capital and Credit Demands in U.S. Agriculture: Projections for Alternative Economic and Policy Environments." Ph.D. dissertation, Iowa State University.

English, Burton C., R. Joe Schatzer, Roland K. Roberts, and Earl O. Heady. 1981. *Potential Long-Term Agricultural Impacts of the Russian Grain Embargo*. CARD Report 97, Ames, Iowa: Center for Agricultural and Rural Development.

Foote, Richard J. 1953. "A Four Equation Model of the Feed-Livestock Economy and Its Endogenous Mechanism." *Journal of Farm Economics*, 35:44–61.

Forrester, J. W. 1961. *Industrial Dynamics*. Cambridge, Mass.: The M.I.T. Press.

Fuller, Wayne A., and James E. Martin. 1961. "The Effects of Autocorrelated Errors on the Statistical Estimation of Distributed Lag Models." *Journal of Farm Economics*, 43:71–82.

Fuller, Wayne A., and James E. Martin. 1962. "A Note on the Effects of Autocorrelated Errors on the Statistical Estimation of Distributed Lag Models." *Journal of Farm Economics*, 44:407–410.

Glickstein, A. A., E. M. Babb, C. E. French, and J. A. Greene. 1962. *Simulation Procedures and Production Control in an Indiana Cheese Plant*. Purdue University, Agricultural Experiment Station Bulletin 757.

Haavelmo, T. 1944. "The Probability Approach in Econometrics." *Econometrica*, 12: Supplement.

Halter, A. N., and G. W. Dean. 1965. "Use of Simulation in Evaluating Management under Uncertainty: Application to a Large Scale Ranch." *Journal of Farm Economics,* 47:557–573.

Heady, Earl O. 1946. "Production Functions from a Random Sample of Farms." *Journal of Farm Economics,* 28:989–1004.

Heady, Earl O. 1981. "Commentary" on "Alternative Designs for Policy Models of the Agricultural Sector" by Stanley R. Johnson. In *Modeling Agriculture for Policy Analysis in the 1980's,* the proceedings of a symposium sponsored by the Federal Reserve Bank of Kansas City, September 24–25, 1981.

Heady, Earl O., and John L. Dillon. 1961. *Agricultural Production Functions.* Ames: Iowa State University Press.

Heady, Earl O., and Luther G. Tweeten. 1963. *Resource Demand and the Structure of the Agricultural Industry.* Ames: Iowa State University Press.

Heady, Earl O., Leo V. Mayer, and Howard C. Madsen. 1972. *Future Farm Programs.* Ames: Iowa State University Press.

Heady, Earl O., Thomas M. Reynolds, and Kenneth H. Baum. 1977. "Tax Policies to Increase Farm Prices and Income: A Quantitative Simulation." *Canadian Journal of Agricultural Economics,* 25:1–14.

Helmers, Glenn A. 1965. "Factors Affecting the Demand for Farm Labor." Ph.D. dissertation, Iowa State University.

Holland, E. P., et al. 1966. "Dynamic Models for Simulating the Venezuelan Economy." The Simulamatics Corporation. Mimeo.

Johnson, S. R. 1981. "A Critque of Simulation Models." *Proceedings of a Conference on the Use of Simulation Models in Agriculture,* pp. 56–67. Kansas City Federal Reserve Bank.

Just, R. and G. Rausser. 1981. "Simulation Models and Forecasting." *Proceedings of a Conference on the Use of Simulation Models in Agriculture,* pp. 46–55. Kansas City Federal Reserve Bank.

Klein, L. R. 1950. *Economic Fluctuations in the United States, 1921–1941.* New York: John Wiley & Sons.

Klein, L., and A. S. Goldberger. 1955. *An Econometric Model of the United States, 1929–1952.* Amsterdam: North-Holland.

Koopmans, T. C. 1950. *Statistical Inference in Dynamic Economic Models.* New York: John Wiley & Sons.

Lin, An-Yhi. 1967. "Factor Demand in United States Agriculture: Econometric Simulation." Ph.D. dissertation, Iowa State University.

Manetsch, Thomas J., et al. 1971. "A Generalized Simulation Approach to Agricultural Sector Analysis with Special Reference to Nigeria." Final Report, Michigan State University.

Minden, A. J. 1965. "Domestic Demand Functions for New Farm Machinery." Ph.D. dissertation, Iowa State University.

Ray, Daryll E. 1971. "An Econometric Simulation Model of United States Agriculture with Commodity Submodels." Ph.D. dissertation, Iowa State University.

Ray, Daryll E. 1973. "The Use of Extraneous Information in the Development of a Policy Simulation Model." *Southern Journal of Agricultural Economics,* 5(1):167–174.

Ray, Daryll E., and Earl O. Heady. 1972. "Government Farm Programs and Commodity Interaction: A Simulation Analysis." *American Journal of Agricultural Economics,* 54:578–590.

Ray, Daryll E., and Earl O. Heady. 1974. *Simulated Effects of Alternative Policy and*

Economic Environments on U.S. Agriculture. CARD Report 46T, Ames, Iowa: Center for Agricultural and Rural Development.

Reynolds, Thomas M., Earl O. Heady and Donald O. Mitchell. 1975. *Alternative Futures for American Agricultural Structure, Policies, Income, Employment, and Exports: A Recursive Simulation.* CARD Report 56, Ames, Iowa: Center for Agricultural and Rural Development.

Roberts, Roland K. 1979. "Analysis of Selected Policy Impacts on the U.S. Livestock Sector by a Five-Commodity Econometric Simulation Model." Ph.D. dissertation, Iowa State University.

Roberts, Roland K., and Earl O. Heady. 1979. *A Five-Commodity Econometric Simulation Model of the U.S. Livestock and Poultry Sector.* CARD Report 83T, Ames, Iowa: Center for Agriculture and Rural Development.

Roberts, Roland K., and Earl O. Heady. 1980. *An Analysis of Selected Agricultural Policy Impacts on the U.S. Livestock Sector by an Econometric Simulation Model.* CARD Report 92, Ames, Iowa: Center for Agricultural and Rural Development.

Roberts, Roland K., Earl O. Heady, and R. Joe Schatzer. 1980. "An Econometric Simulation Model of U.S. Agriculture Used to Estimate Crop Exports Required for Price Maintenance." *Modeling and Simulation: Socio-Economics,* 11 (Part 4):1467–1472.

Schatzer, R. Joe, Roland K. Roberts, and Earl O. Heady. 1981a. *Alternative Futures in U.S. Farm Size Structure, Productivity, Exports, and Income: A Simulation.* CARD Report 99, Ames, Iowa: Center for Agricultural and Rural Development.

Schatzer, R. Joe, Roland K. Roberts, and Earl O. Heady. 1983. "A Simulation of Alternative Futures in U.S. Farm Size." *North Central Journal of Agricultural Economics,* 5(1): 1–7.

Schatzer, R. Joe, Roland K. Roberts, Earl O. Heady, and Kisan R. Gunjal. 1981b. *An Econometric Simulation Model to Estimate Input Stocks and Expenses, Supply Responses, and Resource Demand for Several U.S. Agricultural Commodities.* CARD Report 102T, Ames, Iowa: Center for Agricultural and Rural Development.

Scott, J. T., Jr. 1965. "The Demand for Investment in Farm Buildings." Ph.D. dissertation, Iowa State University.

Scott, J. T., Jr., and Earl O. Heady. 1966. *Aggregate Investment Demand for Farm Buildings: A National, Regional and State Time-Series Analysis.* Iowa State University Research Bulletin 545.

Shechter, Mordechai. 1968. "Empirical Decision Rules for Agricultural Policy: A Simulation Analysis of the Feed Grain Program." Ph.D. dissertation, Iowa State University.

Theil, H. 1958. *Economic Forecasts and Policy.* Amsterdam, Holland: North-Holland Publishing Co.

Thompson, Robert L. 1981. *A Survey of Recent U.S. Developments in International Trade Models.* USDA, Economic Research Service, Bibliographies and Literature of Agriculture No. 21.

Tinbergen, J. 1939. *An Econometric Approach to Business Cycle Problems.* Paris: Herman et Cie.

Tyner, Fred. 1966. "A Simulation Analysis of the U.S. Farm Economy." Ph.D. dissertation, Oklahoma State University.

Tyner, Fred, and Luther G. Tweeten. 1956. "A Methodology for Estimating Production Parameters." *Journal of Farm Economics,* 47:1462–1467.

Tyner, Fred, and Luther G. Tweeten. 1968. "Simulation as a Method of Appraising Farm Programs." *American Journal of Agricultural Economics,* 50:66–81.

United States General Accounting Office. 1977. "Food and Agriculture Models for Policy Analysis."

JOHN L. DILLON

4

Agricultural Production-
Function Analysis

P roduction functions are at the base of production economics. They determine what production is feasible and, within feasible levels of production, they specify what combinations of inputs are rational from a purely physical perspective. Married with information on the prices of inputs and outputs, they guide and determine producers' decisions on the amounts of inputs to be used and products to be produced if producers' goals are to be best achieved. Conversely, every production decision implies some configuration of production functions, prices, and goals held by the producer. This has always been and will always be the basic importance of the production function. With hindsight, this is obvious. That it is now obvious is largely due to Earl Heady.

Not least among Heady's many contributions was to make economists, and particularly agricultural economists, recognize the basic importance of the production function and to actually do something about it in terms of using it as a tool of analysis with ramifications stretching all the way from the individual producer to the market,

John L. Dillon is Professor, Faculty of Agricultural Economics and Business Management, University of New England, Armidale, Australia.

policy, and development arenas. Heady did this in the context of both theoretical and empirical analysis. (Suffice it to note the reception and impact of his *Economics of Agricultural Production and Resource Use* [Heady, 1952] and *Agricultural Production Functions* [Heady and Dillon, 1961]).

Though fully recognizing the contributions of his predecessors, the fact is that it was Heady who fathered agricultural production economics, and particularly production-function estimation and analysis, in their modern form. He who established the production function as a core element of the agricultural economist's bag of theory and put empirical clothes on the theory. For this alone, even without all his other contributions, the profession of agricultural economics will always be indebted to Earl Heady.

What was Heady's motivation in this work? I believe that basically he wanted to make the world a better place and he saw that, within his orbit of influence, a major way of doing this would be to make production more efficient. Ideally, he wanted farmers to know their production functions and use them to be as efficient as possible to benefit both themselves and, through the market, the world. Of course, as Heady well knew, this is an impossible dream. Nonetheless, as is so often the case, it is a dream that provides the impetus for progress and world betterment.

Where are we today with agricultural production-function analysis? To answer we need to look at our production-function theory and its empirical application from the farmer's perspective since it is the farmer's decisions which consummate and determine the relevance of the theory.

Typically the farmer has to decide on some combination of products to be produced from among the set (Yj) of products whose production is physically feasible given the set of input factors (Xi) pertinent to the farm. In the simplest theory it is assumed that production of any product Yj is a known function of a specified set of input factors totally under the farmer's control, that there are no joint products, that production is instantaneous, and that the prices of products and factors are given. It is then straightforward to determine how much of each input factor should be allocated to production of each product and how much of each product should be produced so as to maximize the farmer's profit.

Reality, however, is far different from this simple but basic theoretical model. In general, production functions are not known, many input factors are not under the farmer's control, joint products are not uncommon, production takes time and cannot be predicted with certainty, and product prices are uncertain at decision time. Once these inadequacies of the simple theory were recognized, agricultural economists have endeavored to close the gap between their production theory and reality. In these endeavors Heady again led the way with his seminal consideration both of output and price risk and of activity analysis via mathematical programming as a particular form of production-function analysis to determine the farmer's optimal product portfolio and its associated pattern of factor allocation between products. Indeed, since the publication of *Linear Programming Methods* (Heady and Candler, 1958), time has shown that linear programming and its extensions (including multi-period and risk programming) are by far the most fruitful means of assisting farmers in their problem of determining their production portfolio on a whole-farm basis. In other words, experience indicates that mathematical programming is a far more fruitful approach than classical production-function analysis to the problem of practical planning for multi-product farms. To a great extent, the reasons for this lie in the difficulties that occur in the consideration of a single-product production-function situation. These difficulties, while approachable to a manageable degree in the context of a single product, become unmanageable (relative to the ease of mathematical programming) under the compounding effect that occurs when multiple-product possibilities have to be considered simultaneously. Mathematical programming, of course, does not solve the difficulties. To varying degrees, it merely assumes them away. It does, however, provide a mechanical procedure for handling a mass of activity input-output and price data in such fashion as to provide a first-cut set of "optimal" product combinations and input allocations for producer consideration.

The differences between the simple theory of production stated above and the reality faced by farmers relate to time and risk. Both are always pertinent in the real world. They are absent from the simple theory through its assumptions of instantaneous production and certainty about input levels, output, and prices. Time and risk, of course, go together. Where future time is involved, risk as a result of uncertainty about future states or outcomes must always be present. Only when we can remember the future will risk be absent!

While risk is a consequence of time in the sense that time implies an uncertain future, time itself is also a pervasive influence in agricultural production processes. It directly affects the physical production process, and it also influences the efficiency of production through time-price effects.

There are four ways in which time may affect the physical production process. First, the contribution of fixed inputs may vary with the time-length of the production process. Second, the capacity of fixed inputs to accommodate variable inputs may be a function of time and the mix of variable inputs used. Third, the time-pattern of input provision or output harvest may influence production. Fourth, there may be carryover of variable inputs from one production period to the next. All of these situations imply that time, in some appropriate way, should be included as an input variable in the production function and so it can be influential in determining the optimal levels of production and inputs (including, where appropriate, the optimal time-length of the production process and the optimal time-pattern of input provision).

From a pragmatic point of view, the above considerations imply a variety of possible classifications of production processes on the basis of time considerations. One such classification (Dillon and Anderson, 1990) that has proved useful is in terms (a) of whether inputs are provided at the start of the process or in some (variable or invariable) pattern over the production period with or without carryover effects between periods and (b) of whether there is a single or multiple harvesting of output on some invariable or variable pattern over time.

Time-price effects, quite apart from time-induced uncertainty about prices, arise from two considerations. First, when inputs are tied up in a production process over time, alternative uses of the inputs are forgone and an opportunity cost is incurred. The effect of this is to make inputs (including time) more expensive so that their optimal levels are lower than would otherwise be the case. Second, the fact that production takes time implies the need to allow for time-preference effects of discounting future payments to give comparable present values. Again the effect of this is as of a friction to production and a lowering of the optimal level of input use. Both the above effects of time opportunity cost and preference have been elaborated in the production-function context by Dillon and Anderson (1990).

From a farmer's perspective, the time-related deficiencies of the simple classical production-function approach are probably not too serious. Time-preference effects are only likely to be significant in the context of production processes having production periods of longer than a year. Time-induced opportunity-cost effects are probably of greater relevance since they occur in any production process where the producer has the option of continuing the current run of the process or of terminating the current run by a harvest and starting a new run of the process regardless of the season — as in broiler production or feed-lot fattening of cattle, for example. Probably most relevant of possible time effects on the production process is the matter of the sequencing or pattern of input provision over time. This is particularly important in the provision of irrigation water, in applying fertilizer and other inputs to crops under intensive production, and in the provision of different feed regimes to livestock over time.

Over the last decade the theory of handling the various effects of time as an input and as a source of cost in the production process has been relatively well developed. There is also no shortage of empirical illustrations of the application of these theoretical developments to real-world situations, broiler production and feedlot fattening of cattle perhaps being the prime examples (see Dillon and Anderson, 1990, Ch. 6). As yet, however, it can hardly be said that empirical analysis incorporating such considerations is a matter of routine. One area that stands out as being worthy of further work in the context of production per se is the consideration of time effects in the pasture-livestock grazing production process. Another area, far broader and far more important, is the relation between agricultural production and the environment over time. Much more empirical work needs to be done in this area, looking not just at soil degradation effects arising from such production-associated phenomena as erosion, fertility depletion, and salinization but also at broader effects on the environment. The difficulty, of course, is that most of these effects develop only slowly over time and need long data traces for their analysis. The appraisal of such effects also implies a broadening of production-function analysis away from its traditional emphasis on priced outputs so as to accommodate environmental effects which are generated as unpriced joint products of agricultural production processes.

Risk, like time, also is an inherent feature of agricultural production processes. A tychistic view of the world comes naturally to farmers. Again, just as with time effects, recent years have seen the elaboration of production-function analysis in various ways to accommodate risk considerations. The extensions made include such different procedures as using various non-probabilistic criteria for choice derived from game theory; applying a risk discount factor to possible returns so as to ensure conservative analysis; using the expected value of returns for evaluation; and applying a safety-first rule of requiring some minimum level of profit at some guaranteed level of probability. It also has included using a decision theory approach based on the theorem of expected utility which, given the acceptance of some simple but reasonable axioms related to ordering, continuity, and independence of choice between alternatives says that (a) a subjective probability distribution exists for the uncertain outcomes associated with any risky alternative a decision-maker may face; (b) a utility function exists that reflects the decision-maker's preferences between alternative risky choices; and (c) that the decision-maker's risky choice is optimized by choosing the alternative with the highest expected utility index. The utility approach thus brings together in an explicit way the two crucial elements in risky choice: the decision-maker's personal degrees of belief as reflected in subjective probability and personal degrees of preference as reflected by the utility function.

All of the above-mentioned approaches to risky production may have some relevance for different decision-makers from a descriptive or behavioral point of view. In normative terms, however, they are not equally attractive. The game-theoretic procedures are wrong in ignoring the fact that subjective probabilities can always be ascribed to uncertain events. Though they may have behavioral appeal to some decision-makers, risk-discount factors and safety-first levels are arbitrary and have no logical foundation. The use of expected returns to choose between alternatives implies indifference to risk. Only the decision theory approach based on the maximization of the decision-maker's expected utility is normatively coherent and logical as a basis for risky choice.

In the context of production-function analysis, the essence of the decision theory approach is the application of expected utility maximi-

zation to the probability distribution of profit generated by the production process. In doing this, subjective probability distributions as
held by the decision-maker are associated with all the uncertain variables in the production process. Usually, the most important of these
uncertain variables will be product price and yield. An important
feature of this approach is the recognition that the production function involves three types of input variables: (1) those whose levels are
controlled by the farmer, i.e., the decision variables; (2) those whose
levels are not controlled by the farmer but are known at the time a
choice has to be made about the decision variables, i.e., the predetermined variables; and (3) those whose levels are neither known nor
controlled by the farmer, i.e., the uncertain variables. Only if there is
interaction between the uncertain variables and the decision variables
will the choice of levels for the decision variables be influenced by
yield risk, which, however, will always influence the choice between
the alternative products.

The decision theory approach to production-function analysis
has been rather fully elaborated by Anderson, Dillon, and Hardaker
(1977, Ch. 6) and Dillon and Anderson (1990, Ch. 7). The latter
work also elaborates the joint consideration of risk and time effects. As
a glance at these works shows, the decision theory approach is too
complicated for farmer use. Beyond knowledge of the production
function it also implies knowledge of the relevant probability distributions and of the farmer's utility function. As a way around this difficulty, the use of stochastic efficiency analysis based on the rules of
stochastic dominance has been suggested. In contrast to the identification of the risk-optimal input combination that is possible with knowledge of the utility function, stochastic dominance analysis only identi-
fies sets of risk-efficient operating conditions for decision-makers
whose degree of risk aversion falls within various specified ranges. Its
difficulties lie in its assumption that all decision-makers hold the same
probability distributions and in the complexity of its empirical application (Dillon and Anderson, 1990, Ch. 7). Though less demanding
of data than the fully fledged decision theory approach, stochastic
efficiency analysis is no panacea to the general problem of risky choice
facing farmers.

From this overview of production-function analysis in its simple
form and as extended to accommodate time and risk, what conclu-

sions can be reached? First, it is clear that in its simplest form production-function analysis does not recognize the complexities of the real world induced by time and risk considerations. Nonetheless, if data is available for its use, the simple approach can still be useful as a first-cut guide to farmer decisions on input use relative to individual products. Second, it is clear that from the perspective of a typical farmer, the data demands and analytical complexities of the extended approach accommodating time and risk are too costly to be worthwhile. But for some farmers in some situations — notably large farmers in data-rich circumstances — the extended approach may be worthwhile. Third, while production-function analysis may have advantages for the consideration of individual products, mathematical programming in its various forms is a far more fruitful approach as a guide to multi-product whole-farm planning. Fourth, it is obvious that the effects of location specificity throughout the world in terms of climate, soil, technology, etc., are such that the full array of production functions used by or available to farmers can never be specified. The same is also true for the time considerations, probability distributions, and utility functions associated with these production functions. The best that can be hoped for is that pertinent data and analysis may be available for some major products in some major recommendation domains. This is perhaps a reasonable expectation for some developed countries. To a degree it is probably already true for the U.S. Corn Belt, for example. For developing countries it is probably a less reasonable hope as it implies a research capacity beyond of most of them. Some interesting developments are, however, evident. For example, the development of methods pertinent to the analysis of on-farm trials in farming systems research (see Nordblom, Ahmed, and Potts, 1985) and the development in India of farmer recommendations based on alternative strategies depending on the date of onset of the monsoon.

In sum, therefore, production-function analysis as an approach to the normative solution of the production decision problems of the world's farmers is an unachievable dream. Nonetheless, like all ideals, it provides a fruitful way of looking at the world, giving a better appreciation of farmers' problems and a guide to the ways in which they may be assisted in meeting these problems whether from a research or a policy perspective.

So much for production-function analysis from the perspective of farmers' normative decision-making. What of production-function analysis of a more macro nature as based on cross-sectional farm or industry data? Again this is an area pioneered by Heady. In the past such analysis was frequently used to make deductions about the efficiency of farmers' resource use under such resource headings as land, labor, machinery, operating capital, etc. Such analysis is obviously too gross to be used as the basis for recommendations to individual farmers on their resource use. It may, however, be pertinent in the context of macro modeling of the agricultural sector or of the economy at large. In recent years this approach has somewhat given way to the use of cost and profit functions as duals, respectively, to the production and objective functions of production-function analysis. This has some relative advantages in terms of data needs and simplicity of analysis. However, as noted by Dillon and Anderson (1990, Ch. 4), duality theory implies strong assumptions about farmer behavior and, in its application, remains highly artistic in nature.

Overall, how might agricultural production-function analysis be judged? As I believe Earl Heady too would have argued, it must be seen as one of the important elements of theory and empirical analysis basic to the efforts of agricultural economists as they endeavor to make the world a better place. The more efficient the world's agriculture, the better fed its people can be and the more resources there can be available to satisfy people's needs and aspirations, now and in the future, beyond the essentials of food and fiber.

REFERENCES

Few references have been cited in this lucubration. Readers are directed to Dillon and Anderson, 1990, which lists some 900 references pertinent to the various dimensions of agricultural production-function analysis.

Anderson, J. R., Dillon, J. L, and Hardaker, J. B. 1977. *Agricultural Decision Analysis.* Ames: Iowa State University Press.
Dillon, J. L., and Anderson, J. R. 1990. *The Analysis of Response in Crop and Livestock Production,* 3d ed. Oxford: Pergamon Press.
Heady, E. O. 1952. *Economics of Agricultural Production and Resource Use.* Englewood Cliffs, N.J.: Prentice Hall.

Heady, E. O., and Candler, Wilfred. 1958. *Linear Programming Methods*. Ames: Iowa State University Press.

Heady, E. O., and Dillon, J. L. 1961. *Agricutural Production Functions*. Ames: Iowa State University Press.

Nordblom, T. L., Ahmed, A. H., and Potts, G. R. (eds.). 1985. *Research Methodology for Livestock On-Farm Trials*. IDRC, Ottawa.

JOHN PESEK

5

Isoclines and Isoquants:
Expansion Paths and Substitution Rates

arl O. Heady was born and reared in rural western Nebraska where the productivity of farmland and the uncertainty of production represented serious problems and challenges to the farm people he knew. It would be interesting to know how this caused him to embark on a path which would lead to prominence in agricultural economics, international recognition, and a legacy of economic principles and applications in both plant and animal agriculture. But speculation is not needed to observe the mark he has left on applied agronomy.

His undergraduate training was in both agronomy and agricultural economics and certainly must reflect the concerns of his family during his youth, a time in which a major boom in agriculture was followed by the most devastating of depressions. Such lessons are not missed by young people approaching college age. He completed his undergraduate work during a time when the country was converting from flesh horsepower to mechanical horsepower, and from open-pollinated corn to corn hybrids. These were exciting times; I lived

John Pesek is C. F. Curtiss Distinguished Professor in Agriculture and Professor Emeritus of Agronomy, Iowa State University.

through them, too. There was a great difference in the sophistication of care demanded by horses and mules and the tricycle all-purpose row-crop tractors cultivating two rows at a time at a giddy pace back and forth across the field — and they did not have to be stopped to take a "breather." Early corn hybrids were only a promise of what was to come.

The environment in agriculture was one of new sets of choices among production methods, and the expansion of farms in response to mechanization had begun. Substitutions among production factors became viable options.

Heady's long and successful professional career began in graduate school during the early 1940s. His doctorate degree coincided with the end of World War II, and soon one of the greatest revolutions in agriculture was about to begin. Thus, his professional career began with the waning of the traditional agriculture, altered relatively little until then by farm power mechanization and hybrid corn from what it had been since before the turn of the century.

He taught agricultural economics at Iowa State University, and by the time I heard of him in 1950, he had established a strong reputation in teaching production economics. *Economics of Agricultural Production and Resource Use* (Heady, 1952) became a major text for graduate students in agricultural economics and for graduate students in plant and animal production disciplines who took minors in agricultural economics. In his teaching he presented economic principles in terms of agricultural production, which provided his students with the basis to make sound judgments on the applicability and usefulness of their discoveries in producing the basic raw materials for food and fiber.

An early publication, "The Economics of Rotations with Farm and Production Policy Applications" (Heady, 1948), illustrates both his contribution to the principles of land allocation to various crops on a farm and his emerging interest in agricultural policy. The latter blossomed a decade later with the creation of the Center for Agricultural and Economic Adjustment of which he was the director. Expansion of the scope of the work of the Center beyond the boundaries of the state and beyond simple economic adjustment led to the Center for Agricultural and Economic Development, which became the present Center for Agricultural and Rural Development (CARD), which deals with problems of national and global dimensions. All these creations of Earl Heady and their significance is better addressed by others. Suffice it to say that even for a man of his capacity for voluminous academic and research effort, his work in production agriculture became more limited as Center work became more demanding.

A production economist, once having elaborated the theoretical bases for decision-making and action in an economic sense, is limited in application by the data available. The data in plant and animal production are generated and collected by biological scientists. Up through the late 1940s, agronomic data dealt mostly with the yields of cultivars and hybrids and with the yield of crops grown in rotations of various types. The first publication by Heady that impressed me was a research bulletin entitled *The Economics of Crop Rotations and Land Use* (Heady and Jensen, 1951). Heady and his co-author described it as "a fundamental study in efficiency with emphasis on economic balance of forage and grain crops." The basis for rotations and the choices to be made are that a farmer has the choice of growing several crops either alone in continuous sequence or else in rotations. The study showed that the commitment of a certain acreage of a farm to other crops (basically soil nitrogen-sparing or nitrogen-fixing crops) led to a greater total production of grain on a farm and to availability of the other crops for other uses. Subsequent studies by Heady and his co-workers illustrated how the careful balancing of selected livestock enterprises on the same farm with the crop rotation could be achieved to lead to the highest potential income for the farm.

But the fertilizer revolution was upon us and another research bulletin five years later entitled *Combination of Rotations and Fertilization to Maximize Crop Profits on Farms in North Central Iowa* (Heady, 1956) illustrated how rapidly the options for producing crops changed with the advent of universally available inexpensive fertilizers. By that time, his colleagues in agronomy had shown that plots in a field in continuous corn since 1915, none of which had ever yielded even 80 bu/acre and had averaged less than 50, could be made to produce well over 100 bu/acre. And this could be accomplished with the simple expedient of fertilizing with ammonium nitrate. The United States had a large residual ammonium nitrate manufacturing capacity because this much nitrate was no longer needed for ammunition.

The late 1940s and early 1950s saw many experiments conducted with several rates of nitrogen fertilizer with and without co-varying rates of one or more other elements. Usually the range of rates was not very great nor did the number of rates often exceed three or four. These data were not very satisfactory for the estimation of curvilinear multiple-factor production functions for crops. These kinds of data were not quickly forthcoming because the factorial experimental designs available at the time consumed a large area of land—especially in crops like corn—and, even if confounded, were subject to large experimental error. On the other hand, experiments with animals could be expanded in size and replicated without a similar increase in experimental error.

Heady collaborated with colleagues in animal science on experiments that lent themselves to stringent economic analyses, which led to the formulation of economically optimum rations and feeding rates for several classes of animals, including swine, broilers, turkeys, dairy cattle, and beef (Heady and Dillon, 1961). These feeding schedules were refined to the point of specifying different rations for animals in different stages of growth or production. The concepts of substitution and expansion paths as costs among inputs and the price of output changed were well developed. The lessons learned from the animal experiments made it easier to work with field crop experiments later.

Producers and scientists long have recognized that plants and animals respond to different inputs in their production systems—fertilizers in the case of plants and ratios of amounts of feed nutrients in animals. Near the turn of the century Mitscherlich, in Germany, proposed that the incremental response to fertilizer was proportional to the decrement from maximum yield or

$$dy/dx = c(A - y)$$

which, when integrated, becomes

$$\log A - \log (A - y) = cx$$

where x is the magnitude of the fertilizer being studied, c is the effect factor, y is the yield obtained at any given level of x, and A is the maximum obtainable yield achieved by adding x.

Independently, Spillman in the United States observed that successive equal increments of fertilizer added to a crop tended to form the terms of a decreasing geometric series. This led him to devise the equation

$$y = A - MR^x$$

where A is the maximum yield attainable by adding fertilizer x; M is the maximum yield increase attainable; and R is the ratio of the incremental yield increase resulting from the successive increment of x to the yield increase which results from the previous equal increment of x. The Spillman and the Mitscherlich equations can be shown to be the same.

Both of these equations were difficult to fit to data by the method of least squares, a common procedure used in the analysis of experiments in the 1940s and 1950s. Both Mitscherlich and Spillman showed how the most economical rate of fertilizer use could be calculated. Interestingly enough, agronomists used the Mitscherlich equation almost exclusively to study mineral nutrition of plants, while economists almost exclusively used the Spillman equation to derive economic optima of input use.

Another problem with these equations was that they applied to only one factor varied at a time when it was well known that crops frequently responded simultaneously to two or more elements in fertilizers and that often there was either a positive or negative interaction between the effects of elements. If fitting these equations in a single variable was very difficult, fitting of these equations to data with multiple resource inputs was extremely tedious and time consuming. Besides, these equations are asymptotic to a maximum and thus did not provide for the commonly observed declining yield with excessive applications of nutrients. Mitscherlich did modify his basic equation to account for this, but it was hardly ever used in estimating economic levels of fertilizer use and certainly not for fitting data involving two or more fertilizer elements.

The least square method of analyzing experimental data readily led to the easy fitting of linear and quadratic curvilinear equations and root transformations of quadratic equations. In the single variable form, the quadratic equation is

$$y = a + bx + cx^2$$

where y is the yield, a is the intercept, b and c are coefficients, and x is the fertilizer nutrient. This equation is easily expanded to accommodate another variable fertilizer nutrient, z, and even more as follows:

$$y = a + bx + cx^2 + dz + ez^2 + fxz + \ldots$$

where d, e, and f are additional coefficients and xz is the term providing for interaction or the effect of one nutrient on the response to the other and vice versa.

The multivariate quadratic equation provides for curvilinearity and for diminishing returns to fertilizer inputs, in which case the signs of coefficients c and e would be negative, and for the interaction of the two nutrients, either positive or negative depending upon the sign of f. However, because a curve can fit any three points exactly with no error, the experiments needed to fit these equations required at least four levels of each nutrient, leading to a minimum of 16 or 25 combinations (plots) for four and five levels of each of two nutrient elements, respectively. When replicated, at least the latter set of combinations for a corn experiment would require a land area of an acre or more. This restricted number of rates also had faults: there were limited degrees of freedom for deviation from the regression, and the highest level of nutrient applied would be relatively low or else the spacing of levels would be too great to give the best definition of the response curve in the economically important region of the response surface. This was especially true when zero levels of all inputs traditionally formed the base point of all response curves and surfaces.

The first agronomic experiments attempting to meet the requirements set forth by Heady and still to be practical in terms of execution were conducted by the author in 1951 (Heady and Pesek, 1954). Selected combinations of nine levels of nitrogen and phosphorus fertilizer were applied to corn on a calcareous Ida silt loam in western Iowa and to similar experiments with phosphorus and potassium variables each applied to an experiment on top dressing alfalfa and top dressing red clover on soils in north central Iowa. The array of treatments for the corn experiment is given in Table 5.1. (Substituting K_2O for nitrogen gives the design for the other experiments.)

Table 5.1.   Design of Experiment for Corn; Each "X" Represents an Experimental Plot.

Pounds P$_2$O$_5$ per Acre	Pounds Nitrogen per Acre								
	0	40	80	120	160	200	240	280	320
0	XX	XX	XX	XX	XX	XX	XX	XX	XX
40	XX	XX			XX	XX			XX
80	XX		XX		XX		XX		XX
120	XX			XX	XX			XX	XX
160	XX	XX	XX	XX	XX	XX	XX	XX	XX
200	XX	XX			XX	XX			XX
240	XX		XX		XX		XX		XX
280	XX			XX	XX			XX	XX
320	XX	XX	XX	XX	XX	XX	XX	XX	XX

Source: Heady and Pesek, 1954.
Note: The treatments were assigned at random (completely randomized block design).

Fortunately, the 1952 growing season permitted the highest recorded state average yields of corn up until that time, 52 bu/acre. The highest experimental yields of fertilized corn were approximately 150 bu/acre, and the yield of the plots without nitrogen or phosphorus were on the order of 10 bu/acre, as expected. The data that were collected were excellently suited for fitting of several different response surfaces and subsequent economic analyses. The quadratic surface fitted to the data was

$$y = -7.41 + 0.584N - 0.0016N^2 + 0.664P - 0.0018P^2 + 0.00081NP$$

where P is the pounds of P$_2$O$_5$ per acre and N is the pounds of nitrogen (Heady and Pesek, 1954). The equation displays diminishing returns to both nitrogen and phosphorus and a positive nitrogen by phosphorus interaction which had been previously observed in other experiments on this soil type. A potassium variable was not included because the soils were known to be well supplied with potassium. A graph of the response surface above the 40 lb per acre rates of both nitrogen and P$_2$O$_2$ is presented in Figure 5.1, and a graph of the isoquant and isocline projection is presented in Figure 5.2.[1]

Inspection of the response surface in Figure 5.1 indicates that there are many points of equal yield on the surface and that the same

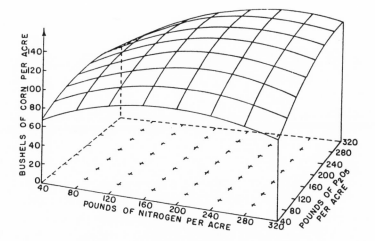

FIGURE 5.1.   Production surface for corn grown
on Ida silt loam as affected by rates of nitrogen and
phosphorus fertilizers. (Heady et al., 1961)

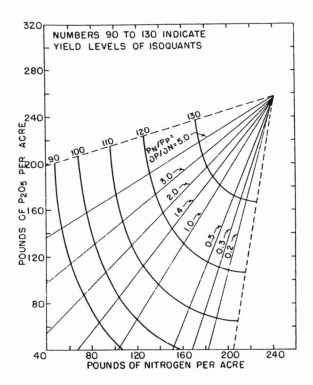

FIGURE 5.2.   Equal yield lines (isoquants) and
expansion paths (isoclines) for corn response surface
in Figure 5.1. Dashed lines are ridge lines. (Heady
et al., 1961)

yield may be produced by the application of different combinations of
nitrogen and phosphorus. It is also evident that there is a maximum
point on the surface with yield decreases measured and estimated in
the original data beyond the maximum yield level. This response
surface, published in "A Fertilizer Production Surface with Specification of Economic Optima for Corn Grown on Calcareous Ida Silt
Loam" (Heady and Pesek, 1954), was probably the first of its kind
ever published and interpreted in the literature.

The isoquants in Figure 5.2 are generated by fixing the yield
level, y, in the yield surface equation and solving for either phosphorus or nitrogen level at an assigned level of the other. It is evident
that 100 bu of corn could have been produced in that experiment with
40 lbs of P_2O_5 and almost 160 lbs of nitrogen per acre or with about
205 lbs of P_2O_5 and approximately 70 lbs of nitrogen per acre or with
numerous combinations between these two.

The isoquants are closed curves representing contours on the
yield surface. All parts of the isoquants lying outside the ridge lines
require more of one or both nutrients to achieve the same yield,
which means that regardless of the relative price of nitrogen to phosphorus fertilizer, the least cost combination to produce any given yield
will be found between the ridge lines. Ridge lines connect points on
isoquants with either zero or infinite slopes and they intersect at the
maximum.

The slope of an isoquant is the ratio of nitrogen to phosphorus
used to achieve the yield at that point, and this is the most profitable
combination for that yield when this slope is equal to the inverse price
ratio of the two inputs. If this ratio changes, production should be at
different points on the isoquant. This led to the term *substitution rate* for
the substitution of one fertilizer nutrient for another. This caused a
degree of disturbance among agronomists because all learned early in
their careers that nitrogen cannot substitute for phosphorus and vice
versa in the nutrition and physiology of the plant. In retrospect, the
use of *substitution effect* might have been a better choice of terms.

The isoclines are drawn by equating the partial derivative of one
nutrient to the partial derivative of the other and equating it to different inverse price ratios of the two. The isoclines connect points of
equal slope of the isoquants. This means that at any given price
ration, say 3.0, one would increase yield most economically moving

from one isoquant to another by moving from the intersection of the isoquant with the 3.0 isocline up to the next isoquant. The interesting effect here is that one would choose a different ratio of nitrogen to P_2O_5 at increasing yields. This concept also produced its problems because one could not simply increase the amount of a certain fertilizer mix to increase yield and do it most economically.

The maximum point in Figure 5.1 or Figure 5.2 is calculated by differentiating the regression surface equation with respect to each fertilizer nutrient, equating each to zero, and solving the two equations simultaneously. In this case, the maximum yield is achieved with about 240 lbs of nitrogen fertilizer per acre and almost 260 lbs of P_2O_5 per acre. The most economical or optimum rate of fertilizer is calculated by equating the partial derivative to the nutrient/corn price ratio for each nutrient, respectively, and solving simultaneously. The solution will always be found between the ridge lines in Figure 5.2 and will approach maximum yield as either the price of corn goes up or the price of nutrients goes down. The optimum rates will recede from the maximum as the price of corn decreases or the price of the nutrients increases.

This work of Heady and his colleagues indicated that the choices of levels of fertilizers to use and the ratios of combinations are very dynamic and change whenever there is a price change in either the inputs or the grain produced. This brings into play a great degree of uncertainty because the relative prices cannot be predicted. The other element of uncertainty is that the production surface changes from year to year—it is not constant.

Heady and his students and colleagues showed how game theory could be used to deal with certain types of uncertainty. This included such devices as maximizing the minimum, solving for minimum regret, or determining action by assessing the subject's ability or willingness to accept risk. One problem with the use of game theory is that it requires a matrix of consequences across various choices that are made. Such data are largely lacking in many agronomic fields, including fertilizer use, and even a series of annual observations of the outcomes is subject to error because of the effect of emerging technology on the outcome. For example, a weather pattern that might have led to a devastating loss due to drought ten or twenty years ago, might very well be less hazardous due to greater drought tolerance of new hybrids (see Walker et al., 1960, for some of this work).

Another way of dealing with uncertainty or doubt about the future is through discounting. Just as the costs of fertilizer inputs can be discounted for the cost of owning the nutrients prior to harvest (adding the interest cost to the price of the nutrient), the returns from the fertilizers can be discounted either by discounting the expected price or the response surface, either of which is easy to do when equations with linear coefficients are used to describe the response surface.

The returns to fertilizer usually are not complete in any one year. In most cases in the Corn Belt, there is a large residual effect of phosphorus applied and there is even a residual effect of the nitrogen applied, although it is usually relatively less. Proper experiments can lead to measuring the residual effect in subsequent years by fitting a regression for the yield for two, three, or more years and then calculating the optimum amount to use with a multiple-year horizon appropriately adding the cost of owning the fertilizer (paying interest for it) during this period (Pesek et al., 1960).

Other applications of production functions to data included the estimation of optimum fertilizer use for crop rotations for which data had been accumulated for a decade or more. It was also shown that the optimum fertilization of perennial crops on an annual basis might be different depending upon whether one, two, or three harvests (such as in hay) were considered or whether the total production for the year was used as the basis (Walker et al., 1963).

Heady and his students also showed how other variables besides fertilizer input (e.g., stand levels of corn) could be combined in yield equations and optima determined. This led the agronomists directly or indirectly associated with Heady's research to develop yield equations based not only upon controlled inputs but also upon uncontrolled inputs (for example, anticipated rainfall) and initial field conditions (initial fertility status of the soils) into the equations (Voss and Pesek, 1962). By this time, computers had the capacity and the ability to fit equations to data with large numbers of variables became easy. In fact, this technical development in computation capacity had a profound effect and made it feasible to expand the possibilities of applying economic principles to decision-making in the production of field crops. These large equations, which included measurements of initial soil tests, were combined in the Iowa State University Soil Testing Laboratory so that the recommended fertilizer applications to farmers based on soil tests continuously reflected the economic climate as well as production potentials. The Iowa State laboratory was the first to do this thanks to the pioneering work of Heady in the field of microeconomics in agriculture.

Joining colleagues in the Tennessee Valley Authority, Heady established and conducted two major national conferences dealing with the economics of fertilizer use and the generation of suitable and needed information for making production decisions based on external inputs. It was during these conferences that the agricultural community became generally aware of rotatable experimental designs which more efficiently estimated the coefficients of quadratic and related types of equations. Other conference participants showed that the principles of rotatable experimental designs could be converted to more practical composite designs for actual field experiments. These designs made it possible to collect better data at more sites than had previously been possible, and thus the knowledge needed to make even better fertilizer recommendations greatly increased.

Just as the optimum rate of fertilizer use maximizes the profit and therefore the upper limit of rational fertilizer application, it is recognized that lesser amounts of fertilizer applied are also profitable and that the average returns to fertilizer are higher (Pesek and Heady, 1958). In an environment of limited capital for farming operations, choices must be made concerning allocation of capital among enterprises. The response equations of Heady and others permitted the allocation of capital resources based on the equating of marginal returns among enterprises requiring variable inputs. Thus, seldom, if ever, would the equating of marginal returns to the inverse price ratio be followed in practice. Profit maximization with limited capital on a farm scale is the objective. But in addition to the variable costs of adding fertilizers, there is a fixed cost. This means that a certain minimum amount of fertilizer must be applied before the return covers both fixed and variable costs up to that point. Given this circumstance, one would forgo the use of fertilizers if this minimum amount could not be applied. This led to the idea of maximizing the return on the total fertilizer input (fixed plus variable cost). This rate, in a profitable situation, then represents the minimum amount of fertilizer to use, and the range between the minimum and the optimum represents a rational operational range for fertilizer application (Pesek and Heady, 1958). This idea is part of the Iowa State University fertilizer recommendation picture.

Heady had a tremendous impact on the thinking of people in agronomy and in agricultural economics and farm management relative to off-farm resource use in crop production. His insight and ability to apply basic economic principles to both risk and uncertainty in agricultural production has been instrumental in fashioning our relationship with the farming and agricultural business clientele in the state. By placing Iowa State in a leadership role in these relationships, others in the U.S. have followed suit. The concept of allocation of resources based upon expectations and initial conditions is very timely and appropriate to the resource enhancement and resource conservation goals being promoted in present-day sustainable agriculture.

An even greater legacy of Heady is the large number of graduate students who studied under his tutelage and countless additional ones who took production economics courses from him or who were fortunate enough to have him as a member of their graduate program of study committees. Students in the biological sciences were introduced by him to concepts of applying the results of their experiments to real life situations in production agriculture.

Students for whom he served as major professor are distributed worldwide. Someone once said that Heady could land at most international airports and be greeted by a former graduate student — and in most cases by several! Thus, his legacy and influence are global and they are perpetuated in his former students and by their students into future generations of scholars. His worth to us and to society is, thus, immeasurable and without limit.

NOTE

1. Isoquants are x-y plane projections of equal yield levels, y, from a production surface. The slopes of the isoquant represent the substitution rates of x for y or vice versa at the same yield levels. Isoclines connect points of equal slopes on isoquants, so they are expansion paths.

REFERENCES

Heady, Earl O. 1948. "The Economics of Rotations with Farm and Production Policy Applications." *Journal of Farm Economics* 30:645–664.

Heady, Earl O. 1952. *Economics of Agricultural Production and Resource Use.* Englewood Cliffs, N.J.: Prentice Hall.

Heady, Earl O. 1956. *Combinations of Rotations and Fertilization to Maximize Crop Profits on Farms in North Central Iowa.* Iowa State Agriculture and Home Economics Experiment Station Research Bulletin 439.

Heady, Earl O., and J. L. Dillon. 1961. *Agricultural Production Functions.* Ames: Iowa State University Press.

Heady, Earl O., and Harold R. Jensen. 1951. *The Economics of Crop Rotations and Land Use.* Iowa State Agriculture and Home Economics Experiment Station Research Bulletin 383.

Heady, Earl O., and John Pesek. 1954. "A Fertilizer Production Surface with Specification of Economic Optima for Corn Grown on Calcareous Ida Silt Loam." *Journal of Farm Economics* 36:466–482.

Heady, Earl O., John T. Pesek, William G. Brown, and John P. Doll. 1961. "Crop Response Surfaces and Economic Optima in Fertilizer Use." Chapter 14 in *Agricultural Production Functions,* ed. Earl O. Heady and J. L. Dillon, Ames: Iowa State University Press.

Pesek, John, and Earl O. Heady. 1958. "Derivation and Application of a Method for Determining Recommended Rates of Fertilization." *Soil Science Society of America Proceedings* 22:419–423.

Pesek, John T., Earl O. Heady, and Lloyd C. Dumenil. 1960. "Influence of Residual Fertilizer Effects and Discounting upon Optimum Fertilizer Rates." *Transactions* 3:220–227. 7th International Congress of Soil Science, Madison, Wisconsin.

Voss, Regis, and John Pesek. 1962. "Generalization of Yield Equations in Two Variables. III. Appreciation of Yield Data from 30 Initial Fertility Levels." *Agronomy Journal* 54:267–271.

Walker, Odell L., Earl O. Heady, Luther G. Tweeten, and John T. Pesek. 1960. *Application of Game Theory Models to Decisions on Farm Practices and Resource Use.* Iowa State Agriculture and Home Economics Experiment Station Research Bulletin 488.

Walker, William M., John Pesek, and Earl O. Heady. 1963. "Effect of Nitrogen Phosphorus and Potassium Fertilizer on the Economics of Producing Bluegrass Forage." *Agronomy Journal* 55:193–196.

WILFRED CANDLER

6

Development and Applicaton of Farm-level Programming Models and Other Farm Management Techniques

The evolution of Earl O. Heady's interest in farm management and production economics is reflected in his early books:

> *Farm Accounting and Records* (Hopkins and Heady, 1949)
> *Economics of Agricultural Production and Resource Use* (Heady, 1952)
> *Farm Management Economics* (Heady and Jensen, 1954)
> *Linear Programming Methods* (Heady and Candler, 1958)
> *Agricultural Production Functions* (Heady and Dillon, 1961)
> *Operations Research Methods for Agricultural Decisions* (Agrawal and
Heady, 1973)

Farm Accounting and Records shows his early concern to know what actually goes on at the farm level and also his characteristic preoccupation with assisting farmers to farm better. There followed Heady's

---

Wilfred Candler is Senior Economist, Development Research Center, The World Bank.

"small blue book," which married the theory of production economics to almost too many empirical examples, many of them already the result of research by Heady and his co-workers. This book was a triumph of the first order. It provided countless agricultural examples of numerical estimates of the theoretical relationships being discussed. It clearly distinguished between decision-making under certainty (when everything is known), risk (in which the probability distributions are known with certainty), and uncertainty (where new information may result from each decision taken). It also illustrated the application of production economics to nontraditional areas such as rental arrangements and regional development/competition. He showed how an understanding of production economics could lead to the redesign of rental arrangements to make both landlord and tenant better off, thus moving this aspect of land economics from a simple description of typical leases into an analytical discipline. This book alone would ensure Heady's high professional reputation.

Farm Management Economics followed. It presented the principles of production economics in a practical setting for both undergraduate students and farmers without the somewhat intimidating size of the Blue Book.

Heady was thus poised for the introduction of linear programming (LP). He was already active in promoting interdisciplinary research to get at the basic technical production relationships; he had a thorough mastery of budgeting and farm record keeping; and he had produced the best exposition of how it all fits together. He lacked, indeed the profession lacked, any way in which we could practically represent production problems in more than two or three dimensions. Thus Heady's "Pork Costulator" was an ingenious analogue method of allowing a feeding ration to balance energy and protein at least cost to achieve a desired rate of gain. Today we would not think of using a Costulator since we can get the answer much quicker from a microcomputer. There were no microcomputers, and budgeting was the state of the art. Enterprise budgeting allowed the profitability of an enterprise to be evaluated. Partial budgeting allowed marginal adjustments to be studied, and whole farm budgeting allowed comparisons of what today we would call scenarios, such as making all the adjustments needed to feed corn on the farm rather than sell it. That was it, and the available computational tools were a pencil, paper, eraser, and an adding machine. Budgeting had no way of identifying a sequence of scarce resources and re-evaluating enterprises in terms of the opportunity cost of using these resources, although the Swedish development of "programming planning" moved budgeting in this direction. The analytical ideas of what needed to be done were readily available in the Blue Book, but a mechanism for doing them cost effectively was lacking.

Thus Heady's article, "Simplified Presentation and Logical Aspects of Linear Programming Technique" in the *Journal of Farm Economics* (December 1954), introduced a whole new field for research. This article combined both a description of the problem to be addressed and, significantly, an exposition of the computing rules for problem solution. An earlier article by Dorfman, "Mathematical or 'Linear' Programming, A Non-mathematical Exposition" (*American Economic Review,* December 1953), had drawn attention to LP as applicable to management problems in an industrial setting but did not give any algorithmic guidance; and a book by Charnes, Cooper, and Henderson (1953), *An Introduction to Linear Programming,* gave computational instructions but in the context of section of a least-cost nut-mix, which hardly helped one see how this should be applied to farm management. There was rapid acceptance of LP by the profession, and papers appeared on dealing with rotations, incorporation of livestock, "lumpy" inputs such as machinery, and so on.

Iowa State was at the forefront of these developments, since Heady saw that "whole farm problems," which previously could only be explored with alternative "scenarios," could now be optimized. Three organizational accomplishments were needed to underpin this line of work: (a) attraction of funding for these studies, (b) attraction of graduate students to take charge of individual studies, and (c) organization of the computing room (this was still the age of pencil and paper) so that problems could be solved efficiently. Students were already flocking to Iowa State to study under him — that was no problem — but many of us may have taken the financial and computational support more for granted that we should have.

The range of applications addressed in this period is evident from the titles of his Experiment Station Research Bulletins (RSB) and other publications:

Combinations of Rotations and Fertilization to Maximize Crop Profits on Farms in North-Central Iowa. RSB 439, with McAlexander and Shrader.

Optimum Allocation of Resources between Pasture Improvement and Other Opportunities in Southern Iowa Farms. RSB 435, with McKee and Scholl.

Optimum Combinations of Livestock Enterprises and Management Practices on Farms Including Supplementary Dairy and Poultry Enterprises. RSB 437, with Gilson.

Optimum Farm Plans for Beginning Farmers on Tama-Muscative Soils. RSB 440, with Loftsgard, Paulson, and Duncan.

An Analysis of Returns from Farm and Nonfarm Employment Opportunities on Shelby-Grundy-Haig Soils. RSB 440, with Dean and Yeh.

Optimum Farm Plans for Beginning Tenant Farmers on Clarion-Webster Soils. RSB 449, with Mackie and Howell.

An Application of Programming to Testing Efficiency of Leasing Systems. I.S.C. *Journal of Science,* with Egbert.

Plans for Beginning Farmers in Southwest Iowa with Comparison of Farm and Nonfarm Income Opportunities. RSB 456, with Mackie and Stoneberg.

Use of a Dynamic Model in Programming Optimum Conservation Farm Plans on Ida-Monona Soils. RSB 475, with Smith.

Adjustments to Meet Changes in Prices and to Improve Income on Dairy Farms in Northeastern Iowa. RSB 430, with Baumann and Orazem.

Analysis of Income Possibilities From Farm Adjustments in Southern Iowa, Including Production of Grade B Milk. RSB 481, with Love.

Profit-Maximizing Plans and Static Supply Schedules for Fluid Milk in the Des Moines Milkshed. RSB 486, with Krenz and Baumann.

Programming Procedures for Farm and Home Planning under Variable Prices, Yield and Capital Quantities. RSB 487, with Loftsgard and Howell.

From RSB 439 to RSB 487 (1956 to 1960) Heady and his students were publishing more than a quarter of the Iowa Agricultural and Home Economics Experiment Station research bulletins on linear programming studies alone, never mind the contributions being made in the context of technical production functions or survey-based research.

This line of work, despite being titled "research bulletins," was extremely practical. It was aimed at top farmers and extension agents and responded to real world problems. In the course of modeling these practical problems, Heady and his students modeled many new situations. Rotations where crop yields depend on the previous use of the land, livestock where the size of the herd is given but can be maintained in several ways, inter-temporal problems where investments need to be tracked over several years, risk where coefficients are stochastic, diverse resource endowments, and supply response were among the many topics on which these bulletins broke new ground.

In looking at, for instance, plans for beginning farmers, we quickly learned that if all resources were increased in proportion, then the ratio of activities in the farm plan remained unchanged. But this led to interest in how the farm plan should change between beginning farmers who were highly capital rationed versus those with more ample supplies of capital. Initially, separate analyses were conducted for each situation, but later it was recognized that by slightly changing the computational rules used, it was possible to trace out plans for all levels of capital with only a small increase in computational effort. Similarly, in looking at a dairy farm plan, we soon realized that the "optimum" farm plan typically remained unchanged for small changes in the milk price. It was a natural development to then ask, by how much would price have to increase in order for the farm plan to change? Again, a small modification of the computational rules allowed us to trace out all farm plans as milk price changed over a predetermined range, producing the well-known "stepped supply function" characteristic of programming studies. These changed computational rules greatly increased the usefulness of LP as a research tool, since the whole production function for a resource or supply function for a price can be traced out. These techniques are now described collectively as parametric programming.

A feature of these pioneering days of LP at Iowa State was that all calculations had to be carried out by hand. Not only did this mean a considerable organizational burden of maintaining a flow of work to the Statistics Laboratory, but anything which could be done to reduce the computational burden was of the first importance. Rereading *Linear Programming Methods* is to enter another world, with a significant chapter on minimizing the computational burden. Row and column checks and a logical structure of calculating only the coefficients actually needed were developed in Ames, and problems were routinely checked for redundant restraints and activities. Even with these refinements, the largest problem which could be handled by hand was about 20 restraints by 40 real activities. Problems of this size could take two weeks to be completed by hand, and prior to the introduction of computational checks, an error on day 3 (if used as the pivot) could invalidate the balance of the calculations. Scissors were a standard part of clerical equipment in the early days to cut off several days work invalidated by one error! The high computing cost had a hidden benefit in that it focused minds on (a) the essence of a problem to be analyzed, (b) compact representation of the problem, and (c) how to get the most information from the fewest calculations.

With the introduction of the computer, Heady was among the first to foresee the day when LP would be tailored to describe an individual farm and used as a management tool by individual farmers. In 1956, he wrote "Mechanical Brain Always Finds Your Best Farm Plan!" for *Capper's Farmer Magazine*. This featured Heady with some of his key students and two farmers looking at some computer output, perhaps the earliest picture of LP results being studied by farmers. He returned to this again with "Next for Farmers— Electronic Planning" in *Better Farming Methods* in 1961 and in a paper to the IBM Agricultural Symposium the following year. This was all long before the advent of the microcomputer and the ability to put electronic planning literally on the farmer's kitchen table.

In pushing this body of work forward, there was a great deal of synergism: Heady exploited economies of scale to the full! Because of his high reputation among agricultural economists, he was able to attract large numbers of students from across the United States and indeed the world. While research contracts imposed some requirements with respect to research outputs, the large body of graduate students meant that in practice it was relatively easy for an individual to mesh his interests with at least one of the topics being studied. Some students wanted to focus on an application, while others wanted to emphasize methodology. This allowed some specialization among graduates, with a body of empirical data to be drawn on, at the same time that "methodological problems" were thrown up in the process of making new applications. Those of us concerned with methodology were given a very stimulating environment in which to work, since if our suggestions were worthwhile there was a ready market for their application.

In my experience, student relationships with Heady varied considerably, depending on their requirements. Some research management was delegated to key senior graduate students, notably Laurel D. Loftsgard, Jerry Dean, and Hal Carter in my day, who monitored the routine aspects of project implementation for him. Heady was particularly active in problem definition, identification of data sources, and presentation of results, and he was available for consultation on problems as they emerged. I never felt any difficulty in getting access to him as my major professor, but also I was very careful to be fully prepared so as not to waste his time. In this environment, he had an incredible capacity to move from one student's concerns to the next. He supported my work actively in terms of identifying data sources or suggesting whom I should approach for further identifying data sources or further help on mathematical or statistical problems. It was clear that he was on top of what I was doing and gave my project considerable thought between meetings. I would feel drained after a 15 or 20 minute interview, but he would keep this up with a succession of students for two or three hours.

I found Heady extremely fair with respect to authorship. It is significant that he sometimes appeared as senior author, sometimes as co-author, and sometimes his name did not appear at all. This reflected a judgement as to how much he had contributed intellectually to the work. If he had conceptualized the project or helped conceptualize it and had helped find the data, then he would usually appear as an author. If, in addition, he had taken the principal part in drafting the paper, he would appear as senior author. His almost endless list of publications was "all his own work." With so many publications, he could afford to let his students get full credit for any work they completed on their own initiative. He also was surprisingly willing to be shown to be wrong (not that this happened very often!), as the following story shows.

In reviewing some work done by an earlier graduate student with Tintner and Heady on LP with stochastic coefficients—a very difficult area—I found that a serious error had been made. The original data provided yields for a range of crops over several years, which could reasonably be assumed to be normally distributed. The student had divided land, labor, and capital requirements by these successive yields to give a series of stochastic input/output coefficients. He had then assumed that these coefficients would be normally distributed, whereas they evidently would be distributed as the inverse of the normal distribution, for which variance is not defined, and the expected value is plus infinity. I prepared a note for the *Journal of the American Statistical Society,* explaining the error and emphasizing the correct procedure, and then asked Heady about publication. He said, "Send it in. Now we know something!" This was typical of Heady's attitude to research. He was open to new suggestions, even if they implied that earlier work could be improved upon. He had no illusion that what we were doing was final and expected that in due course researchers would find ways of improving our work. For him it was sufficient that we were making an important contribution now and using state-of-the-art techniques as they existed at the time. He was not interested in sterile defense of earlier work; rather he was interested in the question How do we do this next study better?

The advent of the computer in the late 1950s, coincided with a shift in Heady's interest from farm modeling to questions involving inter-regional competition and regional models of comparative advantage including environmental costs. This led him to do pioneering work on large LP's but took him away from LP modeling at the farm level. Even Heady could not be on all the research frontiers all the time! It did not, however, dampen his interest in seeing that the industrial methodologies of operations research be exploited in an agricultural context.

In 1973, Agrawal and Heady published *Operations Research Methods for Agricultural Decisions.* This was a very different book from *Linear Programming Methods* or *Agricultural Production Functions,* where Heady was in large measure consolidating his account of a major body of work on which he had been at the forefront. This book represents a useful exploratory account of operations research techniques with potential applications in agriculture. It begins with a brief review of mathematical programming which introduces integer and fractional programming and takes game theory and quadratic programming somewhat further than his earlier book on LP. Agrawal and Heady then review nonmathematical programming topics in operations research, including

1. *Markov chains,* which allow us to project how new technologies, or farm practices, may spread. This is useful to commercial enterprises in seeing how their market share may change, or to extension strategists in seeing how changes in transition probabilities might affect adoption rates.

2. *Queues,* which enable us to analyze how service times will be affected by different patterns of facilities. Rate of acceptance of grain at an elevator, rate of machinery repairs at a dealer, patterns of calls to an extension office, or consultations of a central database are examples of agricultural applications.

3. *Inventory theory,* which has obvious applications in looking at holdings of feed grain, equipment spares on large operations, or for farm supply companies. A less obvious application is in looking at the optimum fodder reserve to hold in drought-prone environments.

4. *PERT, or network analysis,* which is a key tool for the management of any large project — and as such should be a mandatory skill for development economists. It can be used for planning extension campaigns, organizing the local agricultural show, and so forth. It also is a useful subjective management device, since by putting tasks in their logical order, it allows us to identify the "critical path" of events, a delay in any one of which would likely delay completion of the project.

5. *Simulation,* which is particularly useful in analyzing stochastic problems that cannot be put in recognizable form for which analytical or algorithmic solutions are already known. An example would be the study of grazing management, where rainfall (and possible evaporation) affect forage growth, which affects animal growth and is impacted by grazing pressure. Operation of an irrigation system or simple models of market power are other relevant examples.

Farm records, farm accounts, production economics, applied farm management, production function, mathematical programming, other operations research techniques — wherever we look in production economics/farm management — Heady has been there, usually making a major contribution.

Talking of contributions, we should not forget the help which Heady got from enlightened USDA research administrators over the years, and perhaps especially E. L. Baum of the Tennessee Valley Authority (TVA), who collaborated in and supported much of Heady's early quantitative work on fertilizers and related problems.

Finally, one personal recollection about the writing of *Linear Programming Methods* which relates directly to the question, How has one man managed to do so much? It also relates to the vast untapped potential that most people have. I was writing my half of *Linear Programming Methods,* and had been for several months, and had reached a descriptive section on one of the models. Earl and I had agreed on the numbers to be used, and I was simply describing where they came from, how they should be interpreted, and alternative ways of modeling the same structure. For some reason he mentioned to me a couple of times that he would like to see this section. On a Friday afternoon I came down to get my mail before going home and found that he had grown impatient and also had written the section that I had just completed; it was stuffed in my mail slot. The interesting thing is that the two versions were of similar quality and both covered the same topics—but my version had taken me two weeks to complete, while Earl had written his in an afternoon! I also had physical evidence that while I write by the page, Heady wrote by the yellow pad, not even bothering to tear off individual pages.

KENNETH NICOL

7

Applications of
Linear Programming Techniques
to Agricultural Sector Analysis

M any of the professional activities of Earl Heady were directed at the expansion of the frontiers of both the theory and applications of economics in the area of agricultural and resource policy. This was especially true in the area of the application of quantitative methods to the analysis of agricultural policy, management, and adjustment issues. For Heady and his students it was only a small step from the application of programming techniques for the analysis of individual farm and enterprise activity to the combined analysis of the collection of a set of representative farms making up the agricultural sector.

Agricultural sector planning model development, expansion, and use became one of the major activities for Heady and a group of the graduate students he supervised. From their beginning in 1955, these modeling activities expanded in different directions, each with a different focus and capability, and resulted in the Heady System of models. Each of the systems was designed and kept operational with

Kenneth Nicol is Associate Professor, Coordinator, Agricultural Management, The University of Lethbridge, Alberta, Canada.

the intent of providing the student of agricultural policy analysis with an effective tool capable of and compatible with the analysis at hand. As a result of this interrelated but individually focused collection of projects, the Heady System was able to conduct analysis of policy issues in many areas of agriculture with specialized models and support capabilities suited to the needs of the researcher and policy analyst.

The development of the family of programming models in the Heady System allowed the policy analyst to formulate "what if" scenarios for the agricultural sector, thus providing hindsight views of the impacts of proposed policies or programs after implementation. One of the major concerns arising from the use of programming models was, "How do you get from here to there?" It did not take long for the policy analysts using or following the applications of the agricultural sector analysis models within Heady's system to realize that the transition from current to expected state was a significant concern but one which could be handled by policy implementation scheduling and the support systems implemented concurrent with the policy. The main benefit of the programming models was the flexibility to incorporate new technologies and policies into the sector when no prior experience was available upon which to hypothesize change and end result.

The projects for sector planning models were continuously pushing the forefront of available data and computer technologies. Thus it was only at an institution where cooperation and commitment to data collection, system analysis, and computer innovation would go hand in hand with the modeling that the successes of Heady's system could be achieved. Major commitments to data retrieval and processing were facilitated by the cooperation of the USDA offices on campus and the ISU computer center, where commitment to both the latest in computers and the best software for model solution were provided.

THE BEGINNING OF THE HEADY SYSTEM

After years of testing and developing mathematical programming systems at the farm level, planning began for the first sector model based on the census data collected for 1954.[1] The plans called for the definition of the system and the collection of support data for the enterprise budgets prior to the publication of the census. The regional sector production data coming from the 1954 Census of Agriculture were utilized as the basis for the resource (land) availability restraints for the crop production activities in each region. From this beginning the models were extended to include more commodities, more enterprises, more regions, more resource detail, and more output or impact assessment detail for the policies being analyzed. As each generation expanded the database and analytical capability, the foundation was established for the next group of researchers to expand and improve the data and analytical system. This progressional development process is in itself an integral part of the operational system as knowledge and expertise are passed on from the initiators to the followers.

The first model of the system developed by Heady and Egbert[2] was complex in that it provided an analytical capability and detail previously unavailable for analysis of policy and regional comparative advantage in agriculture. However, this initial model had to be considered simple in detail and structure when compared to the land class, farm size, input detail, and analytical sophistication of models developed as the system matured.

The initial model was developed to investigate the impact of several alternative policy and technology options for the wheat and feed grain sectors. The model was to determine the most efficient pattern of grain production based on regional comparative advantage as determined by regional yields, cost of production, and resource availability. The model was cost minimizing in nature, as would be most of the models subsequently developed. The restraints within which the optimization would take place included the wheat and feed grain land base in each of 104 producing areas of the continental United States, and the national demand for the production of food wheat and feed (wheat and feed grains) from all areas.

The model in its first application was used to simulate five different agricultural scenarios. The first reflected a baseline model solved as a minimum cost production system. The subsequent models reflected differing assumptions concerning the resource base, the mobility of land between wheat and feed grain production, the incorporation of a meadow crop in wheat and feed grain rotations, and finally a solution which looked at farm response to local market prices rather than a central or national price.

This initial system illustrated the philosophy that was to come in the development of models incorporating more crops and greater resource and market differentiation. The various systems developed allowed for model responses as a function of cost minimization formulations or profit maximization. When used, the minimization format gave direct measures of resource rents and alternative activity opportunity costs, which are useful information pieces when evaluating farmer production options. The profit maximization systems allowed for the expression of impacts on income and resource values as farmers responded to price signals to change their farming patterns.

THE SECOND GENERATION

The second generation of models in the Heady System began the forecasting format that was to become the major focus of the models in the coming years.[3] This system incorporated cotton and soybeans as well as the original model's wheat and feed grains. Added market detail was provided with the incorporation of 31 demand or consuming regions covering the continental United States. Export totals were allocated to the consuming regions in proportion to historic international trade patterns unless the policy being evaluated would directly influence export patterns in which case those ports directly affected would have export quantities altered accordingly.

The transportation sector was defined as a trans-shipment system between and among these consuming regions. Each producing region had different individual crop acreage restraints which could be modified in response to the assumptions of the agricultural program being simulated. The acreage restrictions which controlled individual crops or crop groups at a proportion of the total available cropland simulated agronomic and/or technical substitution limits in each region.

This formulation of the U.S. agricultural sector model was to become the basic structural format for a series of analyses conducted by researchers and graduate students under Heady's supervision. Each of the analyses was conducted by altering the basic constraint levels reflecting regional resource availability, crop yields reflecting changes in resource productivity or improved seed variety, regional commodity demand, transportation system limitations, and international trade. The intent of these analyses was to evaluate the aggregate effect of government policies,[4] sector capacity, interregional adjustment, and land use,[5] long-term land retirement options,[6] alternative uses for land retired under government programs,[7] and farm policy and rural income and employment.[8]

THE INCORPORATION OF LIVESTOCK

While the crop model was being utilized to analyze the impact of alternative crop scenarios, a parallel activity was under way to incorporate livestock activities into the regional structure of the models.[9] This model incorporated the crop activities of the previous models rearranged into 157 regions which aggregated to 20 demand and livestock production regions. Livestock production activities were defined for milk production, beef cows, cattle on feed, and hog production. Regional shifts in production were allowed within the historic pattern of production capacity and the assumptions of projected changes in these production patterns.

The inclusion of livestock required the definition of additional crop production activities reflecting tame hay and pasture and permanent pasture. Transportation of hay was not allowed outside the demand region in which it was produced. The size of these demand regions would reflect the ongoing activity of local trade in hay but little if any long distance transport of hay. Within the livestock producing regions, the feed requirements are balanced by transformation activities which convert the potential feed sources into feed units and protein requirements.

This model continued to illustrate the great flexibility that can be built into a linear programming framework so that it makes an effective analytical tool for agricultural sector analysis. With each successive model formulated, the detail as reflected in production and transfer opportunities increased. Eyvindson expanded the programming model to the capacity of the computational algorithms at the time.[10]

He built upon the crop and livestock model of Brokken to incorporate farm sizes within each producing region and land capability classes on each farm. This model required data reflecting yield variation by land class and farm size. This required an extensive system of data collection from state and national sources. Also, problems of uniformity of definition and measurement had to be overcome. Because of the volume of data handled, this model development project was among the first to utilize the computer for more than solving the model.

INCORPORATION OF IRRIGATION AND WATER USE

The next major resource expansion within the models was the inclusion of water as a constraint on agricultural production.[11] Expansion of the irrigation capacity of the western states was becoming more expensive and more controversial. Depletion of the groundwater sources in the Southwest was becoming a reality, and the excess capacity of American agriculture was creating an environment within which the development of additional water sources and/or interbasin transfers of water for agriculture was being questioned. Within this political environment the Heady models were modified at the request of the National Water Commission to reflect agricultural production within a set of regions based on contiguous counties which are identified as closely as possible with the water resource subregions of the major river basins of the continental United States. These producing areas aggregate to consuming regions which control demand and transfer of commodities and to water supply regions which control the supply and transfer of water for agricultural use.

This modeling effort was the first of the Heady systems to be fully computerized from the data collection and analysis, commodity production budget and resource restraint generation, commodity demand calculation and allocation to demand regions through to the summary and report table preparation. This computerization greatly facilitated the speed of model development and the reliability of the repetitive calculations in budget development and solution analysis. A great deal of software developed in conjunction with this and subsequent models was capable of relating components of production costs used to calculate the objective function coefficient, and the levels of change in regional activity as solution parameters were changed in response to alternative policy, resource, or demand shifts.

INCORPORATION OF ENVIRONMENTAL FACTORS

With the support of the National Science Foundation (NSF) the sector model incorporating water supplies was expanded to incorporate soil loss and fertilizer sectors to allow for the analysis of soil conservation and nitrate fertilizer use policy options.[12] This environmental model utilized the regional production and consumption delineation developed for the water model described above. In each producing area a maximum of nine soil capability classes were delineated for each region based on either dryland or irrigation farming techniques. The fertilizer component was developed to reflect yield-determining functions which were region, soil class, and fertilizer application level sensitive.

Modeling systems at this level of detail require extensive cooperative activity among technical experts in many fields. The development and application of these systems within the institutional framework of a land-grant university greatly facilitated the access to knowledgeable professionals in the disciplines related to soils, animal husbandry, hydrology, fertilizer use, nitrate sources and leaching, and farm chemical pollution potential. Also, the access to the USDA through the Economic Research Service offices provided contacts to their source of data and contacts to other government agencies.

This model was subsequently used as the basis for a study for the Environmental Protection Agency (EPA)[13] and for the National Water Assessment (NWA).[14] The EPA study investigated the impact and potential adjustment problems within the agricultural sector of proposed agricultural soil loss and nitrogen fertilizer application limitations. The NWA study looked at water availability and water quality as factors which impacted on total and regional agricultural output and sector adjustment potential. The NWA study incorporated a series of regional crop and livestock production shift restrictions which were designed to reflect historically exhibited regional flexibility in commodity production shifts over time.

This series of three projects (NSF, EPA, and NWA) institutionalized the modeling system within a cooperative arrangement with the USDA's Economic Research Service and Soil Conservation Service; these two agencies cooperated extensively in collecting data used to refine soil capability class information for the model. This revised information emphasized land-capability class productivity, sensitivity, and availability by aggregated sub area.

When modeling systems become as complex as this system, extensive data collection and management systems must be in place. It was only through the cooperation of the two USDA agencies and the Bureau of Reclamation in the Department of the Interior that the data for these models could be collected at the level of detail and accuracy that was achieved. Also important in this effort was the computer center at Iowa State University; it provided sufficient access to the computer and the technical and software support which allowed for the development of the data management system and solution of the models.

REVISIONS TO THE ENVIRONMENTAL AND
RESOURCE USE MODELS

A continuation of the cooperation between CARD and the USDA followed these models as the Soil Conservation Service initiated a major expansion of the model to serve as an analytical base to meet the reporting requirements of the Resource Conservation Act. The outcome of this project was the Agricultural Resource Interregional Modeling System (ARIMS).[15] This model encompassed extensive revisions of the NWA and EPA models within the framework of an integrated data management, solution, and reporting system. It encompassed detailed crop, livestock, and range production sectors which interacted with the land use and water and irrigation resource sectors and which were driven by an integrated national and regional demand and transportation system.

It was during the development of this system that Heady's professional career was abruptly halted. This model served as a final reminder of the commitment of Heady to the system he developed as the well-trained staff and the committed working relations he had developed with other institutions, especially within the USDA, were able to continue and see the project through to completion.

Even while the perceived emphasis of the CARD sector modeling program was centered on the major agricultural resource and environmental projects, numerous other projects were still being pursued with derivatives of the operational models in CARD.

A MODEL OF GRAIN TRANSPORTATION

The continued increase in grain marketing and the stress on the capacity of the national grain transportation system which resulted by the early part of the 1970s was the impetus for a modification of the basic grain models to incorporate a detailed transportation network reflecting 78 possible hubs (73 consuming or export regions and 5 dedicated export regions) of an interrelated rail, truck, and barge transportation system.[16] This structure allowed for competition between the rail, truck and barge modes on either short or long haul routes. Also available were mixed mode grain transportation options.

A modeling system which directly incorporates a detailed transportation sector recognizes the role of the transport of the commodity in the market place. Transportation analysis is important when the commodity is transported in such volumes that any change in the regional production or consumption patterns can have profound impacts on the transportation sector or when the physical characteristics or unit value of the commodity are significant in its market analysis. Generally, transportation is more important for commodities that are costly to transport, i.e., that are heavy, bulky, require special conditions, or have a low unit value. Most agricultural products when evaluated in the framework of current transportation networks are not impacted significantly by the transportation sector. However, when major policy revisions are planned for the transportation sector, then the impact of the relative comparative advantage between regions in agriculture may shift. This is the facet that this study investigated.

As with all initial model systems developed by Heady and his staff, the transportation model highlighted as many challenges for future enhancement of the analysis as it answered current questions.

Specific in this instance was the need for improved transportation cost functions and for the development of storage and seasonality characteristics of the commodities being analyzed.

APPLICATIONS TO RURAL INCOME AND EMPLOYMENT

As with most analytical systems the analysis has to be restricted to the specific area of study defined. Most of the applications of the models were directed at the impact on the agricultural production or resource sectors. Only indirectly was any reference made to the impact on the nonproduction sectors of the rural community. Sonka and Heady implemented a study which utilized the regional production models to indicate possible shifts in production patterns in response to policy changes in the agricultural production sector and extended the impact to the income and employment impacts on the nonproduction rural sectors as well.

To determine the employment and income impacts, the solutions to the agricultural production models were linked to a set of secondary income and employment variables to trace policy responses. These impacts had increased activity forecast in three areas: (1) The income received by producers, (2) income received by the agricultural support sectors from the sale of inputs or the processing of products, and (3) income received from the increased sale of consumer goods to farmers as a result of their increased income. The employment impact can be similarly calculated and compared under different policy alternatives.

REGIONAL ANALYSIS WITHIN A NATIONAL FRAMEWORK

In many cases the desire for state or regional action on resource use or environmental protection will require an impact analysis which incorporates the interaction with the larger national market. The national agricultural models available as part of the Heady System were adapted to facilitate the analysis of regional policy or adjustment issues at a detailed level for the region while still allowing for the impact of the national market within which the local policy must be implemented.[17] Huemoeller, Nicol, and Heady investigated a policy of soil loss restriction and alternative rates of land conversion from agriculture in the North Central States. The emphasis being on the trade-offs in regional production as farmers in other regions are not required by the law to implement similar erosion control measures or as specific trends in land diversion from agriculture affects the north central region's production potential as a part of the national framework. The interregional shifts in production are more profound than in situations where all producers nationwide are required to comply. A state-level analysis of soil loss impact reflected similar disproportionate adjustment as the impacted region's producers adjust to the higher cost or more limiting production possibilities in competition with other producers unaffected by production alternatives.

TATONNEMENT MODELING

One of the last major model development activities undertaken by Heady and his staff was the incorporation of a linear program into a recursive or tatonnement system of analysis.[18] This interactive solution system would allow the demand-determining system to settle on a market price and quantity which fit closely with the imputed supply quantity and prices in the production model. By allowing the system to cycle through the estimation of demand and supply prices and quantities an equilibrium solution can eventually be approximated.

CONCLUSION

This system of models developed under the supervision of Heady is still being updated, expanded, and used by CARD. And this must stand as a tribute to its effectiveness and usefulness as much as any listing of the numerous publications, reports, and graduate students that emerged from the system projects to enhance the profession of agricultural economics. The collection of models which made up what I refer to as the Heady System track the profession's capacity to use mathematical tools as a means of supporting analysis of emerging public concerns. As the analysis of policy issues progressed, the development of the models and their capacity to analyze these concerns was evident in the evolution of the Heady models. Also evident in these modeling endeavors was the continual use of computer capacity and software capability to facilitate expanded model analysis and/or more effective and efficient solution of existing models.

I would like to close this summary with a reflection on some of the aspects of being one of the number of graduate students who developed professionally and personally within the environment created by Heady. My first exposure to the modeling system was Heady's assignment of my research assistantship to help on the analysis of policy options looking at alternatives to the land set-aside and storage policy of the Commodity Credit Corporation. This experience began in front of a "Friden" mechanical calculator filling in page after page of commodity demand estimates. When I finished these calculations you can hardly imagine the excitement when I was asked to rerun all calculations with a different parameter on consumption or exports. Only those of you who have used these calculators hour after hour can appreciate the relief when the demand and resource availability sectors were computerized.

I still recall the times when those of us working on the projects would reminisce about computer crashes, lost data files, trips across the United States searching for data, meetings in Washington with congressional or senatorial panels, trips to professional meetings to present results, and all night computer sessions as deadlines approached for project reports. Being a part of a group of researchers who interacted with professionals in many disciplines gave us the insight of the need for and benefits that accrue from interdisciplinary research. We could not have achieved our results without significant interaction from soil scientists, agrologists, crop scientists, water resource specialists of all professions, computer specialists, and environmental specialists.

Heady taught us more than the ideas required to be professional modelers and policy analysts. He taught us understanding for the views of other professionals and interest groups. He taught us discipline both for ourselves and for our profession. He taught us commitment to a project and the need for that commitment to be based on professional and personal ethics. And he provided us the environment within which to practice these lessons and a role model by his behavior to see that they work in the everyday world.

NOTES

1. Alvin C. Egbert and Earl O. Heady, *Regional Adjustment in Grain Production: A Linear Programming Analysis,* USDA Tech. Bull. 1241; Supplement to Technical Bulletin No. 1241, June 1961; Alvin C. Egbert, Earl O. Heady, and Ray F. Brokken, *Regional Changes in Grain Production: An Application of Spatial Linear Programming,* Agr. and Home Econ. Exp. Sta. Res. Bull. 521, Iowa State Univ., Ames, Jan. 1954.

2. For further information of this model see Alvin C. Egbert and Earl O. Heady, *Regional Adjustment in Grain Production: A Linear Programming Analysis,* USDA Tech. Bull. 1241, June 1961.

3. See Earl O. Heady and Norman K. Whittlesey, *A Programming Analysis of Interregional Competition and Surplus Capacity of American Agriculture,* Agr. and Home Econ. Exp. Sta. Res. Bull. 538, Iowa State Univ., Ames, July 1965.

4. See Norman K. Whittlesey and Earl O. Heady, *Alternative Economic Effects of Alternative Land Retirement Programs: A Linear Programming Analysis,* USDA Tech. Bull. 1351, Aug. 1966.

5. See Earl O. Heady and Melvin Skold, *Projections of U.S. Agricultural Capacity and Interregional Adjustments in Production and Land Use with Spatial Programming Models,* Agr. and Home Econ. Exp. Sta. Res. Bull. 539, Iowa State University, Ames, Aug. 1965.

6. See Howard C. Madsen and Earl O. Heady, *Trade-offs in Farm Policy,* CAED Report 32, Center for Agricultural and Economic Development, Iowa State University, 1968.

7. See Howard C. Madsen, Earl O. Heady, and Kenneth J. Nicol, *An Analysis of Some Alternatives for the Future,* CAED Report 34, Center for Agricultural and Economic Development, Iowa State University, Apr. 1969.

8. See Steve T. Sonka and Earl O. Heady, *Income and Employment Generation in Rural Areas in Relation to Alternative Farm Programs,* North Central Regional Center for Rural Development, Iowa State University, Dec. 1973.

9. See Ray F. Brokken and Earl O. Heady, *Interregional Adjustments in Crop and Livestock Production: A Linear Programming Analysis,* USDA Tech. Bull. 1396, July 1968.

10. See Roger K. Eyvindson, Earl O. Heady, and Uma K. Srivastava, *A Model of Interregional Competition in U.S. Agriculture Incorporating Consuming Regions, Producing Areas, Farm Size Groups and Land Classes,* Ames: Iowa State University Press, 1975.

11. See Earl O. Heady, Howard C. Madsen, Kenneth J. Nicol and Stanley H. Hargrove, *Agricultural and Water Policies and the Environment: An Analysis of National Alternatives in Natural Resource Use, Food Supply and Environmental Quality,* CARD Report 40T, Center for Agricultural and Rural Development, Iowa State University, June, 1972.

12. See Ken Nicol, Earl O. Heady, and Howard C. Madsen, *Models of Soil Loss, Land and Water Uses, Spatial Agricultural Structure, and the Environment.* CARD Report 49T, The Center for Agricultural and Rural Development, Iowa State University, July, 1974.

13. See Howard C. Madsen, Ken Nicol, and Earl O. Heady, "Environmental Impacts and Costs in Agriculture in Relation to Soil Loss Restrictions and Nitrogen Fertilizer Limitations," a report prepared for the Environmental Protection Agency, Washington, D.C., November, 1973.

14. See Anton D. Meister and Ken Nicol. *A Documentation of the National Water Assessment Model of Regional Agricultural Production, Land and Water Use, and Environmental*

Interaction, Center for Agricultural and Rural Development Miscellaneous Report, Iowa State University, 1975.

15. For an overview of this model see Burton C. English, Elwin G. Smith, Jay D. Atwood, Stanley R. Johnson and George E. Oamek, *Resource Conservation Act Analysis: An Overview of the CARD Agricultural Resource Interregional Modeling System,* Center For Agricultural And Rural Development, CARD Technical Report 89-TR11, Iowa State University, 1989. For more detail on specific aspects of the model see any of the detailed sector reports described in the above report.

16. See Jerry A. Fedeler, Earl O. Heady and Won W. Koo. *A National Grain Transportation Model,* Center for Agricultural and Rural Development, CARD Report 40T. Ames, Iowa. 1975.

17. See William A. Huemoeller, Ken Nicol, Earl O. Heady, and Brent W. Spalding, *Land Use: Ongoing Developments in the North Central Region,* Center for Agricultural and Rural Development. Ames: Iowa State University Press, 1976. Or see U.S.S.N. Nagadevara, Ken Nicol, and Earl O. Heady, *Implications of Full Application of Soil Conservancy and Environmental Regulations in Iowa with a National Market Framework,* CARD Report 57, Center for Agricultural and Rural Development, Iowa State University, Ames, June 1975.

18. See Burton C. English, Cameron Short, and Earl O. Heady, *Tatonnement Modeling: A Variation to Linear Programming,* Center for Agricultural and Rural Development Miscellaneous paper, Iowa State University, Ames, 1981.

LUTHER TWEETEN
LEO V. MAYER

8

Long-term Agricultural Development and Price and Income Policy

Professor Earl O. Heady's professional role in farm policy differed from his earlier role in production economics. In production economics, he was the dominant intellectual, with pioneering ideas and techniques. In policy, his role was more that of entrepreneur and coordinator. He was especially successful in attracting financial resources, sponsoring conferences and workshops, and publishing proceedings. Numerous publications originated from the Center for Agricultural and Economic Adjustment and later the Center for Agricultural and Rural Development, both of which he headed. The publications, many from the Iowa State University Press, were authored by a wide range of policy experts and dominated the farm and rural policy literature for years.

Professor Heady's intellectual contributions to agricultural policy, although less dominant than in production economics, were nonetheless important and enduring. We begin by outlining his personal

Luther Tweeten is Anderson Professor of Agricultural Economics, Department of Agricultural Economics and Rural Sociology, The Ohio State University. Leo V. Mayer is Senior Analyst, General Accounting Office, U.S. Congress.

perspective on policy, then turn to his major intellectual contribution—articulation of the process of transforming agriculture during the nation's economic development.

Heady's lifetime spanned a period of unprecedented structural transformation in agriculture of a magnitude never to be repeated. It was a period of massive chronic disequilibrium, with redundant labor backed up on farms for years. On farms, it was a time of productivity growth, considerable poverty, underemployment, family farm consolidation and loss, migration to cities, and growth of large farms. In rural areas, it was a time of economic and population decline, school consolidation, and general restructuring. Because Professor Heady cared deeply about people, especially about disadvantaged people, perhaps it is not surprising to see a tinge of populism run through much of his policy writings.

In his teachings and his writings, Professor Heady repeatedly emphasized that productivity advances had driven down real farm prices and incomes, and that farmers deserved compensation for accepting technology that had diminished agricultural income while enhancing the nation's economy. In that spirit, he noted that "the [federal] payments and program costs have been directed toward compensation of farmers, *mainly commercial operators* [emphasis ours] for reduced revenues when greater production pours into a market of inelastic demand" (Heady, 1969, p. 196). Even today some economists view commodity programs as compensation to farmers for adopting new technology. Heady realized, earlier than most, that the compensation was going inequitably to the gainers rather than to the losers. He recognized that programs had "left aside numerous groups in the rural community, and even on farms, who suffer losses under progress of agriculture and subsequent decline in the number of farms and farm workers."

Unfortunately, the problem of directing adjustment and welfare assistance to "farm labor freed for use elsewhere in the economy" or "left stranded in farming . . . at a level of living inconsistent with the degree of wealth and economic growth in the U.S. economy" (Heady, 1961a, p. 77) was never resolved. Commenting on commodity policies "where gains are tied to resources owned and volume produced by farmers," Heady (1975, p. 5) goes on to add,

Not only were mammoth payments transferred from the taxpaying public to large landholders whose central occupation was not farming (while poverty-level farmers were left with meager benefits), but the payment system itself encouraged larger and fewer farms and the consequent erosion of employment and social services throughout many rural areas.

The major agricultural policy problem, in Heady's view, was how to overcome inequities in the distribution of gains and losses of progress from farm structural change (Ball and Heady, 1972, p. 383). Noting the tendency of public policy to encourage centralization, he and Ball stated that

the mix of public farm policies that promotes such new technologies as the mechanization of cotton production or provides large subsidy payments for compensation and land diversion by cotton producers only speeds growth of larger farms, depopulation of rural areas, and migration of unskilled laborers to urban centers as well as creating a vast multiplication of economic and social complexities in the central city. (P. 376)

He recognized the limits of economic analysis and the role of goals and values in finding solutions to farm problems. Exceptional insight was apparent in his preface to *Goals and Values in Agricultural Policies* (Heady, 1961b):

Solutions to the major economic problems must have their roots in goal-value phenomena. The basic economic and physical cause of the agricultural problem is now well understood. Agriculturists and economists can suggest a half dozen ways to solve it. But solutions immediately confront problems in goals and values, the deeply imbedded beliefs of particular individuals, groups, and organizations in respect to "what is right" and "what ought to be."

Some of Earl's own values are apparent from his statement with Gordon Ball:

In terms of our own personal biases flavored a bit with nostalgia for farming, we would favor mechanisms which at least would restrain farm size maximally and farm numbers minimally to a level which allows attainment of the major cost economies of major technology (i.e., to a point on the average long-run cost function where the slope is small and further increments in size bring unimportant reduction in factor costs). This structure would imply modestly large but efficient family units of the "one-unit" size. It would generally exclude the multiplications of this size into large or mammoth units. (Ball and Heady, 1972, p. 387)

AGRICULTURE UNDER ECONOMIC DEVELOPMENT

The dominant theme in Heady's policy writings is the change in agriculture induced by national and international economic development. His most extensive evaluation of the process as it applied to the United States was in his book *Agricultural Policy under Economic Development* (Heady, 1962).

Professor Heady began that volume with the observation that "history will prove that problems of agriculture follow a definite pattern over time and under economic development." His follow-up chapters on goals and criteria for agricultural policy and the role of the political process in resolving conflicts among farm interest groups make interesting reading more than a quarter century later. Many leaders of developed countries continue to struggle with the periodic excess commodity supplies, burgeoning government costs, and the persistent social problems that arise in rural areas as the transformation of agriculture proceeds.

For the United States, these problems became especially evident a decade after the end of World War II. Heady early recognized the role of technological change, capital accumulation, and changing input and output prices during development processes. The resulting technological treadmill, resource fixity, and induced innovation concepts used to explain economic disequilibrium problems of agriculture were precursors to theories subsequently made famous by other agricultural economists.

In a superb article entitled "Basic Economic and Welfare Aspects of Farm Technological Advance" published in 1949, Heady provided an intellectual foundation for understanding the impact of technological changes on agriculture. He noted that output-increasing scale-neutral technology (e.g., biological forms such as improved varieties) has a very different impact on agriculture than has the relatively output-neutral scale-biased technology (e.g., mechanical forms such as the tractor and its complements). Although his book *Agricultural Policy under Economic Development* and earlier writings contained pieces of these and related ideas, the following quote from *Resource Demand and Structure of the Agricultural Industry* (Heady and Tweeten, 1963, p. 13) provides a succinct summary:

> Improved technology introduces new and improved inputs which have high productivity relative to conventional resources. Consequent structural changes in resource demand and production functions increase the supply of products. In industries such as agriculture characterized by a low elasticity of commodity demand, the increasing product supplies depress prices and signal the need to transfer resources from agriculture to other sectors. If resource supply conditions permit rapid introduction of highly profitable and productive capital inputs and prohibit rapid outmovement of less productive resources such as labor, returns to the latter may be chronically depressed. Also, conditions associated with economic development and structural change create pressures for farm consolidation.

American agricultural technological change was of modest pace and was scale-biased toward saving labor in the 1800s. Heady noted that progress was slow in earlier years because science and industry were not well developed but relatively tight labor supplies called for labor-saving technology. As nonfarm industry and land-grant universities improved farm technology in response to demand by farmers, the pace of change quickened. Reviewing a graph showing declining ratios of machinery and other purchased input prices relative to farm labor wage, Heady and Tweeten (1963, p. 88) observed that "from 1930 to 1960, mechanical capital was rapidly substituted for hired labor, . . . directly replacing farm labor of family members." Based on studies of actual farms, Hoffman and Heady found that this process of freeing farm labor and consolidating farms increased farm output. That is, the consolidating new operator realized higher crop yields and livestock productivity than had the operator who exited the farm.

In addition to observing the contribution of public research, Heady recognized the growing importance of agribusiness in enhancing farming productivity during the process of economic development:

The private sector now makes an immense contribution to growth in knowledge of new agricultural technology. This growing investment by the private sector is encouraged especially at high stages of development where the major portion of farm inputs turns to capital. The private sector then has the much larger market mentioned earlier in supplying inputs to agriculture, as compared to lower stages of economic development. Future economic development will be associated with continued efforts of the private sector to extend knowledge of the agricultural production function.

In a small volume of lectures titled *Agricultural Problems and Policies of Developed Countries* published in 1966 by the University of Oslo in Norway, Heady anticipated that other countries would encounter problems as agricultural development proceeded. In his inimitable style, he outlined the agricultural problems associated with development, their sources, and their effects over time:

> The first, reflected as the surplus problem with the tendency of output and commodity supply to progress faster than consumer demand for food, arises because the new forms of capital lift the restraint of land and allow supply to be more elastic. This problem source is so much more obvious that the second problem source tends to be overlooked as an equally basic and less transitory effect of economic development. The second, the relative change which takes place in resource prices under economic development with its effect on the proportion or mix in which resources are employed in agriculture, has further expression in cost economies which attach to the size of the producing unit. Hence, it affects the number of farm units and families which can exist in a competitive "nongrowth" industry like agriculture.

Declining farm numbers and rural populations are at the heart of the international "farm problem" in numerous countries. As presently framed, the overt problem is manifest in agricultural trade disputes. Nations with excess agricultural production compete with subsidies for limited markets in other countries. Commodity programs designed to preserve family farms have become the major trade distortions.

An example is the European Community. By implementing a Common Agricultural Policy of border protection after its formation in 1957, the European Community protected its farmers from foreign competition. In turn, commodity prices were held at high levels to delay the structural transformation of agriculture. The consequence has been venting of European Community farm problems to other countries through export of surpluses. The practice in turn has led to skirmishes with competing exporters and breakdown of the Uruguay Round of trade liberalization negotiations under the General Agreement on Tariffs and Trade.

The analysis that Heady provided in 1966 to the faculty at the University of Oslo in Norway forewarned of this type of problem. The encroachment of the European Community into traditional U.S. export markets is directly the product of trade policies but is indirectly the result of misguided commodity programs. Such misguided programs are in part the product of misguided economic diagnoses of the causes and appropriate cures to farm problems.

EMERGING THOUGHT ON FARM PROBLEMS UNDER ECONOMIC DEVELOPMENT

Heady fit many pieces into the complex jigsaw puzzle that came to be known in the United States as "the farm problem." During his most intensive period of analysis, it was a problem related mainly to the farm, with aggregate input and output that were too high and prices and incomes that were too low by some sociopolitical standard. Most importantly, it was a *long-term disequilibrium problem* endemic to agriculture under economic development—with technology growth outstripping demand growth and with farm labor unable to adjust rapidly enough without severe hardship. By the 1970s, however, evidence began to emerge that excess resources were declining as demand growth exceeded technology growth. Excess labor had sharply diminished.

Farm problems can be viewed in two broad perspectives—as economic equilibrium and as economic disequilibrium. Until quite recently, the latter was the conventional view, the one into which Heady's pieces fit.

The Farming Economy under Long-Term Economic Disequilibrium

Disequilibrium theories hold that farm economic problems arise from the nature of the slope and of shifts in demand and supply for farm output. Central to the theory is identifying those forces (a) that give rise to disequilibrium and (b) that inhibit dissipation of that disequilibrium.

Major sources of demand shocks are (a) weather abroad that along with trade, macroeconomic, and other policies abroad shift U.S. export demand; (b) domestic and foreign economic growth; and (c) domestic business cycles which in the post World War II period have been replaced by "man-made" inflation and other macroeconomic policy–induced cycles as shifters of demand and prices.

The demand curve faced by the farming industry in aggregate and for most commodities was viewed by Heady as inelastic so that small supply shocks brought large changes in price (elasticities he cited of −.4 to −.5 for domestic demand [Heady, 1949, p. 301] seem high by today's standards). The demand curve facing the individual producer is perfectly elastic. Hence, in contrast to producers in less competitive industries, the farmer cannot adjust output to reduce or raise industry price. Heady emphasized that as technological progress caused output to expand against an inelastic demand and revenue falls, less productive and profitable inputs such as farm labor had to adjust out of farming.

Heady (1962, p. 5) also concluded that, because of the low and declining domestic income elasticity of demand and because of macroeconomic policies to avoid depression,

> the major problems of the industry no longer can be framed as those of agriculture in an unstable economy. Great fluctuations and insecurity, such as that illustrating the 1930s, no longer characterizes national economic endeavor. True, small recessions have prevailed since World War II and will continue to do so. But mass unemployment will never be allowed to return. Even under national instability of magnitudes experienced in postwar years, farm income has suffered little, and sometimes not at all.

Heady was probably reacting to T. W. Schultz's 1945 book, *Agriculture in an Unstable Economy,* which gave the traditional business cycle a central role in directly creating domestic demand shocks damaging to agriculture.

Former President Harry Truman once said those who can't stand the heat should stay out of the kitchen. Technology and normal vagaries of nature creating uncertainties from weather, pests, disease, and productivity advances require change which might be viewed as normal "heat" farmers and markets can bear without government interventions. Change induced by price and other incentives giving rise to sustainable gains in productivity not greatly in excess of demand growth might be viewed as tolerable to farmers and a reasonable price to pay for greater economic efficiency and real national income growth.

In case of monetary, fiscal, and trade policy, however, governments play a major role in creating unnecessary uncertainty and change in agriculture. Change induced by improper macroeconomic policies in the 1970s and 1980s was cyclical. The farming economy began a recovery in 1986 that continued to the end of the decade. Even if farm and national income averaged over the economic cycle is as high as farm and national income without the cycle, the changes induced by the cycle are socially traumatic. Many farmers lost in the period of high real interest, and exchange rates are not retrieved when real interest and exchange rates return to normal lower levels. It is important to observe here that conditions in agriculture have changed. The economic cycles characterizing the farming economy in the 1970s and 1980s do not give rise to *chronic* low average prices or rates of return to farm resources, or to *chronic* low farm income.

Heady (1967, Ch. 1) noted changes in the nonfarm economy (in addition to technological treadmill change in agriculture) as a source of farm resource disequilibrium.[1] In his view, capital accumulation and technological change in the nonfarm sector raise earnings of nonfarm workers and hence the opportunity cost of farm labor and management. To maintain some semblance of equality, farms must grow in scale and decrease in numbers in proportion to the rising opportunity cost of labor. Tweeten (1984, pp. 24, 25) found that rising opportunity cost of farm labor to be the second most important source (after technology) of increase in farm size for the 1940–79 period. The factor is not likely to be a large source of farm disequilibrium in the future because (a) the pace of growth of real income per capita of nonfarmers has slowed and (b) the change is gradual and predictable enough for farmers to adjust.

The demand for adjustments described above explain persistent low returns in agriculture only within the context of lethargic supply of adjustments. Heady (1949, pp. 313, 314) listed four obstacles to mobility:

1. Lack of knowledge. Too few know where to go and the level of income to be expected were they to leave agriculture.

2. Cost of transfer. The direct expense of migration, loss of income during the period of transfer, and investment loss from resources reduced in value by reorganization inhibit mobility.

3. Risk and uncertainty of returns. Heady (p. 314) stated that "the feeling of greater security on the farm is ingrained in farm persons to an extent that many prefer a smaller return in agriculture to a higher mean (nonfarm) income." This is similar to John Brewster's (1961, pp. 129ff) endodermal hypothesis explaining the farm problem, which holds that a farmer has a low reservation wage, accepting a low return for labor rather than leaving friends and relatives.

4. Inflexibilities of human capabilities. An individual with family responsibilities may be unable to take time out to acquire skills needed for alternative employment.

Heady's list of obstacles to adjustment and concept of a resource reservation price again anticipated Glenn Johnson's fixed asset theory, which held that assets were fixed "when it doesn't pay to vary them" (Johnson and Quance, 1972).

Adjustments to technological change were made mostly by youth not yet established in farming. Research cited by Heady (1962, p. 455) found that among all occupational groups in 1952, 16 percent of persons whose fathers were farmers were employed as nonfarm proprietors, managers, and officials, a percentage exceeded only by persons whose fathers were in these professions. Farm migrants were high achievers and took their place in nonfarm society with honor, dignity, and accomplishment. Subsequent analysis confirmed that conclusion. Tweeten and Brinkman (1976, pp. 88–92) reviewed several studies indicating that persons established in farming who migrated to the city improved themselves on subjective grounds (they said they were better off) and on objective grounds (income and housing improved along with educational, medical, and other services).

The Farming Economy Nearing Long-Term Equilibrium

A central theme of Heady's work, that the economic problems of agriculture change as national economic growth progresses, implied that many of his and other economists' conclusions regarding farm problems would need to be revised over time. That indeed has happened.

Total aggregate farm input volume remained nearly constant from 1920 to 1990. This implies that no significant resource adjustment would need to have occurred over that period if the farm birth rate would have been low enough only to sustain the farm population and if new technology would have been scale neutral. Demand gains approximately offset supply gains due to productivity. Greater productivity allowed ever lower real farm prices to cover all resource costs of farming. The parity ratio fell but not as much as productivity rose. Coupled with off-farm earnings and expansion in farm size, the trend in recent decades has been towards parity in income per person between the farm and nonfarm sectors despite notable setbacks such as in the mid-1980s.

Mechanization, especially the tractor and its complements, displaced millions of farm workers. The force of that technology was beginning to be spent by the 1980s. In 1989, Tweeten contended that labor and aggregate productivity gains no longer exceeded the capacity of farm resources to adjust, that adequate-size commercial family farms were on average receiving at least as favorable returns as like resources in the nonfarm sector, and that even small part-time farms were earning "socially acceptable" returns because low farm returns were compensated by psychic and tax benefits derived from farming. The implication was that the farming industry was in long-term economic equilibrium,[2] having overcome the disequilibrium created by technology and economic growth in excess of what the sector could absorb for half a century. Of course, problems remain of annual and cyclical instability in the food and fiber sector, and of the environment. Farm outmigration and family farm demise have slowed to a trickle compared to earlier decades. A farming economy characterized by annual and cyclical instability and environmental problems but not by long-term economic disequilibrium requires a very different set of policies than called for in earlier decades. Theories explaining real and apparent farm problems along with appropriate public policies for a farm economy no longer characterized by chronic disequilibrium are discussed at length elsewhere (Tweeten, 1989).

SUMMARY AND CONCLUSIONS

Earl Heady made seminal contributions to the farm policy debate in the United States and in Europe. His contributions include the sources of disequilibrium (technology, national economic growth) and explain why disequilibrium was not quickly dissipated. His contributions endure and are a rich part of the literature in our field.

His principal contribution was to recognize that the form and substance of farm and rural problems change as national economic growth proceeds. He argued at length that policies and programs must also change as economic development proceeds.

A central question of farm policy is not whether shocks create disequilibrium (they do) but whether farmers have capacity to adjust to those shocks so that adequate-size, well-managed farms on average will earn returns comparable to those elsewhere. Empirical findings provide compelling evidence that contemporary American agriculture adjusts rather rapidly to economic disturbances and that adequate-size, well-managed farms tend to earn incomes and rates of return at least comparable to income and returns on like resources elsewhere (see Tweeten, 1989, Ch. 4).

The agricultural economy is no longer characterized by the chronic disequilibrium problems of excess labor and farm consolidation prominent in Heady's time. However, agriculture will continue to experience problems of annual and cyclical instability and of the environment.

NOTES

1. The treadmill theory held that (1) improved technologies were turned out year after year; (2) then were rapidly and unavoidably adopted by farmers; (3) which expanded supply pressing against an inelastic and slowly expanding aggregate demand for food, thereby reducing prices; (4) farm conventional resources needed to be reduced in response to lower returns but were not responsive to prices; resulting in (5) price depressing surplus production year after year except in wartime (Cochrane, 1965, p. 116).

2. An economy is always in short-term equilibrium but never fully reaches long-term economic equilibrium. The term "long-term equilibrium" as used here is only near equilibrium.

REFERENCES

Ball, A. Gordon, and Earl Heady. 1972. "Trends in Farm and Enterprise Size and Scale." In A. Gordon Ball and Earl Heady, eds., *Size, Structure, and Future of Farms*, pp. 40–58. Ames: Iowa State University Press.

Brewster, John. 1961. "Society Values and Goals in Respect to Agriculture." In Center for Agricultural and Economic Development, *Goals and Values in Agricultural Policy*, pp. 114–137. Ames: Iowa State University Press.

Cochrane, Willard. 1965. *The City Man's Guide to the Farm Problem*. Minneapolis: University of Minnesota Press.

Heady, Earl. 1949. "Basic Economic and Welfare Aspects of Farm Technological Advance." *Journal of Farm Economics*, 31:293–316.

Heady, Earl. 1961a. "Nature of the Farm Problem." In Carlton Christian, ed., *Adjustments in Agriculture—A National Basebook*, pp. 54–84. Ames: Iowa State University Press.

Heady, Earl. 1961b. "Preface." In *Goals and Values in Agricultural Policy*, pp. v, vi. Center for Agricultural and Economic Development. Ames: Iowa State University Press.

Heady, Earl. 1962. *Agricultural Policy under Economic Development*. Ames: Iowa State University Press.

Heady, Earl. 1966. *Agricultural Problems and Policies of Developed Countries*. Oslo, Norway: University of Oslo.

Heady, Earl. 1967. *A Primer on Food, Agriculture, and Public Policy*. New York: Random House.

Heady, Earl. 1969. "Developing Economically and Politically Consistent Policies: The Problem of Equity." In *Food Goals, Future Structural Changes, and Agricultural Policy: A National Basebook*, pp. 195–216. Center for Agricultural and Economic Development, Ames: Iowa State University Press.

Heady, Earl. 1975. "The Basic Equity Problem." In Earl Heady and Larry Whiting, eds., *Externalities in the Transformation of Agriculture: Distribution of Benefits and Costs from Development*, pp. 3–21. Ames: Iowa State University Press.

Heady, Earl, and Luther Tweeten. 1963. *Resource Demand and Structure of the Agricultural Industry*. Ames: Iowa State University Press.

Hoffman, R. A., and Earl Heady. 1962. *Production, Income, and Resource Changes from Farm Consolidation*. Agricultural Experiment Station Bulletin No. 502. Ames: Iowa State University.

Johnson, Glenn, and C. Leroy Quance. 1972. *The Overproduction Trap in U.S. Agriculture*. Baltimore: Johns Hopkins University.

Schultz, T. W. 1945. *Agriculture in an Unstable Economy*. New York: McGraw-Hill, Inc.

Tweeten, Luther. 1989. *Farm Policy Analysis*. Boulder, Colo.: Westview Press.

Tweeten, Luther. 1984. "Causes and Consequences of Structural Change in the Farming Industry." NPA Report No. 207. Washington, D.C.: National Planning Association.

Tweeten, Luther, and George Brinkman. 1976. *Micropolitan Development*. Ames: Iowa State University Press.

LAUREN SOTH

9

Income Compensation
and Farm Supply Control

arl Heady challenged the agricultural policy of the United
States on grounds that it distributed gains from agricultural
productivity to consumers but distributed the costs to farmers.
He said this in the early years after World War II, a time of especially
high praise for the accomplishments of the public agricultural research and development establishment. Advancing farm productivity
was lowering the cost of food, permitting a growth in exports and
rapidly reducing the labor force and number of families in farming,
freeing young farm people to meet increasing demand for workers in
urban jobs.

Heady's analysis was rather heretical to be uttered within the
sacred precincts of the land-grant agricultural college system. The
system was founded on the premise that improved farm productivity
would benefit farm people, which was and continues to be its selling
argument for public appropriations. But Heady said this was no
longer the case. He said farm people were entitled to special compensation from the public for what the agricultural development system
was doing to reduce their aggregate income. Not many dared to be so

---

Lauren Soth is a retired editorial page editor of the *Des Moines Register.*

blunt about it. Heady even questioned the allocation of members of his own economics profession to agriculture. In his book *Agricultural Policy under Economic Development* (Ames: Iowa State University Press, 1962), he wrote,

> It is perhaps unfortunate, in the allocation of scarce societal resources, that the public has several thousand economists and other scientists assigned to the agricultural industry, computing quantities to determine its efficiency, increase its productivity and extend the transfer of resources out of it, with hardly a handful directly assigned (as in the manner of public research institutions) to other sectors of the economy where the majority of human and capital resources are invested. Certainly the same resources would allow closer attainment of the social optimum if more of them were allocated to lowering the cost of housing and medicine to the relative level of food; in extending research and facilities for the large number of persons whose psychiatric moorings retard their output and utility level; in increasing the quantity and quality of education and other means for a fuller expression of human capabilities; in improving the abilities and allocation of a large body of unskilled labor; in improving the effectiveness of industrial plants and layouts; in tackling the problems of monopoly; and in lessening inputs for purely neutralizing advertisement in industries of imperfect competition.

Heady was saying that the agricultural industry is afflicted with over-capacity, not just in land and capital resources but also in scientific and educational resources. The benefits to the public from further lowering of food costs are not equal to the costs in reduced welfare of farm people and of progress foregone in other fields because of over-allocation to agriculture. Society would be better off if it put less emphasis on increasing the yields of crops and livestock and devoted more brainpower to improving housing, medical care, and productivity in nonagricultural goods and services.

That is a radical idea. Agricultural research and extension (technical development) have held a place of high honor and near-religious devotion in the United States. To suggest that we are overdoing this work in the land-grant agricultural colleges must be regarded as blasphemy.

The thought that the economic disadvantage of farmers in much of this century stems from excessive public investment in the industry seems wildly unbelievable, indeed unpatriotic. Must agricultural research be appraised as simply one aspect of science, to be evaluated pragmatically in relation to other scientific effort? Can it be true that in attempting to do good for the people on the land, we have done them harm?

Of course these questions arise from the same emotional source as questions about ideology or religion. If a thing is good, such as enabling farmers to produce more at less cost, then there is no limit to the good you should do. Agricultural gains are sacred and cannot be placed in the same context with gains in the profane aspects of living, such as better urban transit or improved hospital care. Agriculture merits public (socialized) management and support more than other occupations.

Agricultural economists and political leaders have long seen the problem of over-capacity in the farming industry. They have recognized that the inelastic demand for food makes further gains in food supplies in rich societies bad business for farmers. Thus the stress on exports and "feeding the world." Few have been ready to argue that farm producers are entitled to special compensation outside the market for providing the public with plentiful food of high quality. Hardly anyone dares say that scientific talent and training should not be allocated so strongly to agriculture.

In *Agricultural Policy under Economic Development* Heady speculated about why food is not a free good in such a rich society as the United States. A visitor from Mars, he said, might find it perplexing that education is provided mostly free and allocated apart from prices while food is not. Why are services such as fishing and hunting and national parks provided mostly free when food is not? Why are postal communications socialized? Why is electricity a public utility? "Why in general have so many goods of secondary or tertiary nature been placed in the category of public utilities when a primary good has not."

Heady thought the reason such policy came about may have been that society could not foresee the level to which economic progress, especially of agriculture, could be pushed. The founding fathers may have supposed that the main preoccupation of man always would be food. "Hence, rather than make agriculture a public utility and provide a minimum quantity of food at zero price to all consumers, an alternative but quite similar policy has been followed.

Food itself has not been socialized or made into a public utility, but resources causing its supply to increase and its real cost to decline were so treated."

But it was largely an "unwitting process and outcome. . . . Research and development as a social or public activity were undertaken with focus on greater income or benefit for farmers. . . . Early legislators, administrators and farmers had little knowledge of price and income elasticities of demand." Not just *early* legislators et al.: the focus of agricultural research, so far as its public justification is concerned, remains about the same as in the early days.

The policy of food development, Heady wrote, "is a noble and worthy policy. It has been efficiently pursued in the United States, and the returns to American society have been great." But is this policy of old still noble and worthy? "It has become necessary to distinguish between the gains to consumers of future generations and gains and losses of farmers in this generation."

Payments to farmers from the public purse may be viewed, according to Heady, (1) as pay to compensate them for the lessened income caused by society's investment in greater production under conditions of inelastic demand for food, (2) as an equity measure to bring per capita farm income up near the level of the nonfarm sector, or (3) as pay to offset the benefits obtained by less competitive sectors through market power. But to accomplish this, payments should be "devoid of any relation to units of output or input used in future periods."

That is what is now called "decoupling." Unless this is done, said Heady, the payments will draw an "overage" of resources into agriculture and of products on the market. That prediction was borne out by the effects of the target-price payments in the 1980s.

The most economical way of shielding farmers from the consequences of excessive production may not be the most acceptable politically. Huge government outlays for agriculture in the 1980s were a major factor in farm policy — turning one wing of the political spectrum toward elimination of farm subsidies and another wing toward production control as a means of helping farmers earn fair incomes in the market place.

Implicit in the Heady analysis of the macroeconomics of agriculture is the concept that public-financed research and education are focused too heavily on the domestic farm industry and agri-industries.

As a corrective, reducing the public investment in the public agricultural institutions relative to other scientific and educational investment would be logical. Another policy move to lower agricultural production capacity in this country could be the diversion of domestic agricultural development efforts overseas. Professor Heady himself was highly devoted to foreign agricultural development in later years. The political obstacles to large-scale foreign agricultural aid have increased during the economic decline of American agriculture during the 1980s. Farmers and their lobbyist-leaders have objected to helping foreign producers of food and fiber become more self-sufficient and more competitive in world markets. Yet there is much evidence to show that raising incomes of people by improving agriculture in the less-developed countries results in increased food imports by those countries. Countries with 70 to 80 percent of the population engaged in farming can raise incomes only by improving agriculture. Higher income increases demand for higher-quality foods, hence larger imports.

For those who want to maintain the structure and size of American agriculture and its related supply and marketing industries, the logic clearly is to divert public research and development to less-developed countries. This tends to build export markets for American farmers—and for agricultural input producers.

The tremendous success of the land-grant agricultural colleges and research stations have been accompanied by growth of agribusiness with a parallel expansion of private research in technology. This has created surplus capacity in these related commercial agri-industries: too much of a good thing for the domestic economy and society of the United States. Therefore, public action to turn more of this highly successful food-and-nutrition-development apparatus to less-developed, low-income countries seems a sound world economic policy.

Certainly it would be profitable for America to develop increased demand for food in poor countries. This, paradoxically, can best be done by helping those countries improve their own food-production industries. The same process—increased agricultural subsidies in low-income countries, plus increased sales of U.S. farm products and agribusiness goods and services there—would reduce surplus pressure and support farm income in the United States and reduce the need for public compensation to American farmers.

SHASHANKA BHIDE

10 810

The Science of
Agricultural Economics in India:
Implications of Heady's Contributions

T
he challenge of alleviating poverty and hunger and of achieving self-sufficiency in an essential commodity—food—has
commanded the attention of various scientists and economists ever since the beginning of the planned era in India. Even
before this, the subject received considerable attention in economics,
especially after the 1926 report of the Royal Commission on Agriculture. However, since the beginning of economic planning, both theoretical and empirical research in agricultural economics has had
greater vigor.

With the establishment of agricultural universities in the pattern
of the land-grant colleges in the United States, agricultural economics
began to be recognized as an important independent field of research.
It is interesting to note that while major research in macro-agricul-
tural economics continued to be done outside of the agricultural university–agricultural research institution complex, the latter focused

Shashanka Bhide is Associate Director, National Council of
Applied Economic Research, New Delhi, India.

attention on micro-level and sectoral-level problems. Bhagwati and Chakravorty (1971) note that "largely because agriculture is the overwhelmingly important economic activity in the economy and its role as the supplier of wage goods to other sectors has been increasingly appreciated, this sector has also attracted considerable economic analysis." The macro issues such as agrarian reform, rural poverty and hunger, nutrition, surplus agricultural labor, and availability of wage goods continued to be discussed and debated in the context of planning for development.

Within agricultural universities, the agricultural economist was occupied with his role as an adviser to the farm-level decision-maker in evaluating alternative farming techniques and in reorganizing the farm activities on more profitable lines. The job was clearly more daunting because of the inaccessibility of clientele to the advisers as well as the need for more interdisciplinary studies with a role for the social scientist, which was just beginning in the early 1950s. It also was challenging since it was often necessary to show that the tools borrowed from the West were equally suitable to the underdeveloped agriculture of India.

The establishment of agricultural universities in the land-grant university pattern, naturally, had resulted in significant American influence on the research and academic activities in agricultural sciences in India, including the area of agricultural economics. This is not to ignore the early studies in agricultural economics and the studies done outside the agricultural university complex. It was recognized in the early 1960s that there were serious data gaps as well as a lack of rigorous and objective studies in agricultural economics which would have to be filled for delivering useful prescriptions for policy. To quote a noted Indian agricultural economist,

> The bulk of the studies in the field of agricultural economics in India are, however, still either of the descriptive or philosophical type and are not sufficiently analytical or functional in character. This is obviously an unsatisfactory situation for there is much greater need now, when we are seeking to accelerate the economic development of our country through a process of economic planning, than ever before for analytical studies and planned purposive research designed to assist in the correct formulation and implementation of the Plan. (Sen, 1959)

The need for analytical studies and the advent of programs for collecting relevant information motivated the researchers to look for an appropriate training framework. While the scholars trained abroad began their work on production functions and farm planning research, the appearance of several pathbreaking articles and textbooks made the task easier for the agricultural economists in India to produce the desired analytical type of studies. In this context, Earl Heady's papers (for example Heady, 1946 and 1952a) and textbooks (Heady, 1952b; Heady and Candler, 1958; and Heady and Dillon, 1961) have marked a definite turning point in the teaching of agricultural economics in India's agricultural universities.

The major areas of agricultural economics pursued are production economics and credit and marketing. Certain special papers are often included on India's agricultural economy and the major economic issues facing the nation. In teaching agricultural production economics as applied microeconomics, it was essential to have workable examples and procedures to demonstrate the use of economic tools to solve farm problems. Heady's textbooks filled the void felt in the early years of agricultural economics in India, and even today these books have continued to be the major texts in the agricultural universities. In a small survey of 11 Indian agricultural universities conducted by this author, all said that the three Heady books on agricultural production functions (1961), linear programming methods (1958), and agricultural production economics (1952) continue to be used as major references in teaching and research.

Further specialization, sophistication, and new areas of application have now been possible because of the basic foundations provided by the past research in which Heady's contribution was fundamental. The rigor in analysis both in theory and method has been a hallmark of Heady's work.

In this chapter, I attempt to capture the essence of Heady's work for the development of agricultural economics in India in the areas of (a) the multi-disciplinary approach in agricultural economics research, (b) agricultural production functions, (c) mathematical programming models in agriculture, and (d) graduate school education. Clearly, Heady's work has encompassed a wide range of issues and methods. Also, the agricultural economics research in India has covered quite different but vital areas within an Indian context: planning and evaluation of agricultural development projects, and agrarian reforms and other institutions in agriculture. But our purpose is limited to the few areas noted above.

The multi-disciplinary research in agriculture and the role of economics in this research came to be recognized when the process of transferring laboratory information to the farmer's field began and the need for economic evaluation of new technology was increasingly felt. A brief look at the topics covered by Heady's enormous research output would indicate the need for a close understanding of agriculture itself and illustrate the interdisciplinary outlook: soil conservation, water and land use in agriculture, energy use in agriculture, crop and livestock production functions, machinery and labor in farming, capital in agriculture, and agriculture and the environment. The topics emphasized the possibilities of using analytical techniques to evaluate problems faced by policymakers in agriculture. Simultaneously, they also underscored the need to have a sound knowledge of agriculture and inputs from fellow scientists—the agronomists, soil scientists, plant breeders, animal nutritionists, and agricultural engineers. This ability to provide useful research input into policymaking also led to a sustained relationship between policymakers and the researcher.

In the Indian context, where agricultural universities have specific regional coverage, the scientists are in a position to recognize the problems specific to their regions and to suggest practical or feasible remedial measures to the policymaker at the regional level. The wide range of agro-climatic and economic conditions prevailing in the country necessitate region-specific analysis, and the agricultural universities are particularly equipped to conduct such analysis. Both multi-disciplinary research and region-specific research could be carried out more easily within the framework of agricultural universities.

Heady's work, while dealing with a range of subjects, emphasized the need for relevant data. To fulfill this need, multi-disciplinary work had to be carried out. The research on agricultural production functions—both crop and livestock, concerned with the use of inputs such as fertilizers and water in the case of crop production and feeds in the case of livestock—was done almost continuously under his supervision. The results, generated while providing the basic data required for advising the producer farmers, also helped analysis in a larger context of sectoral implications.

In India, both water and fertilizer have been critical inputs in crop production. Production-function studies have been carried out since the early 1960s (Raj Krishna, 1964, for instance), but their systematic use in providing recommendations to farmers or policy-makers appears to be limited. This is somewhat surprising given the importance of these factors. The production-function studies in live-stock are even fewer. The importance of Heady's work in this area was recognized by the early researchers in India. In one of the pio-neering applications of production functions for milk in India, Jacob et al. (1969) noted, "Problems relating to the feed substituting rates and least cost rations fall in the domain of agricultural production economics. Most of the recent developments in this field have been due to Earl O. Heady." With greater attention now given to livestock production, and more so with milk production, the need for objective assessment of input-output relationships has become even greater. Well laid out experiments capturing variations in feed inputs, breeds, and climates are necessary to provide information to the producer on how to best utilize his scarce resources.

In the agricultural production-function studies, the experimental data has received greater attention in Heady's work than the farm-level data. In India, some studies using farm-level data were carried out in the early 1960s (Hopper, 1965; Raj Krishna, 1964) but there have been relatively few since then. This may be due to some meth-odological issues related to estimation of production relationships from survey data (Dey and Rudra, 1973). The primary object of estimated production function was to test the rationality of resource allocation by farmers. The more recent applications of cost and profit functions appear to have overcome the estimation difficulties basic to the production-function approach, but they are based on an assumed maximization model. Estimation of these models, however, requires observation of variations in input prices paid by farmers in order to use these functions to obtain production-function coefficients. In In-dia, where inputs such as fertilizer and to some extent water belong to the genre of an "administered price sector" and price variations are relatively minor, this approach has certain limitations. Pooling of cross-sectional and time-series data may diminish the difficulty, but the problem is inherent and the direct estimation of production coefficients by using some alternative techniques needs to be pursued. The data collected for the cost-of-cultivation surveys have now been used to estimate the cost and profit functions, but their use to derive production-function coefficients is less prevalent. The basic data relating to the rates of substitution between inputs (mainly water) and fertilizer in the case of crop production and feeds in the case of livestock production will be increasingly important in the future because these are relatively expensive inputs in Indian agriculture. In this context, drawing upon the research methods adopted by Heady and Dillon (1961), Hexem and Heady (1978), and Heady and Bhide (1983) to provide an overall framework for the planning, estimation, and application of agricultural production functions would prove to be extremely useful.

And yet another area favored by Heady for analysis is the interregional competition models of land and water use based on linear programming methods. Regional specialization for efficient use of resources would be a clear indication of the method. However, the use of restrictions on such specialization helped the models to provide "realistic" solutions. Clearly, the choice of the model was based on the range of problems that could be analyzed using it as well as the economic interpretations that could be attached to each result. A variety of issues ranging from output supply restriction policies, fertilizer use, water use, energy use, soil conservation, and export alternatives were analyzed from a policy perspective.

In the Indian context, considerable effort has been made to derive farmers' responses to economic incentives (acreage response functions and more recently cost-profit function studies) and the results indicate that farmers do respond to these incentives as predicted by economic theory. Askari and Cummings (1976) provide an excellent review of the acreage models. The assumption related to regional specialization needs to be tempered by restrictions on the extent of such specializations as indicated by the model results. The problem related to the "linearity" of the relationships will need to be solved with support from production-function studies. The utility of such models can be even greater when we consider the increasingly felt land and water constraint in Indian agriculture. Several linear programming models have been estimated and used for analysis both at the farm level and the sectoral level in the past (some early applications are

Desai, 1960; Jai Krishna, 1961; and Randhawa and Heady, 1966). But they have not been maintained and updated for continuous analysis over a period of time. This appears to be the case even with econometric models of agriculture in India. It was often felt that short-term future analysis was more realistically captured through econometric modeling than by linear programming models. It is only in recent years that the forecasting models of agriculture and the planning sub-model of the Planning Commission have begun to be used on a continuous basis in India.

The final area covered in this chapter is the teaching-research environment to which Heady's graduate students were exposed. The graduate students working under Heady provided the essential input and were a major infrastructural support for his research programs. The programs offered both an opportunity and challenge to the graduate students. Heady nursed his students, encouraged them, and helped them in numerous ways. Above all, Iowa State University, the seat of Heady's activities, had excellent Departments of Economics and Statistics in a distinguished College of Agriculture. The university also had an excellent computer facility.

The financial support accorded through research assistantships attracted graduate students to Heady both from within the United States and abroad. A strong international representation at Iowa State, more so among the graduate students of Heady, was a normal feature. All this provided both quality and variety. The lecture hall where Heady taught resembled the United Nations assembly in its makeup. The ability to draw a continuous stream of graduate students helped in undertaking sustained research activities over the years. The students added new ideas and provided extensions to the existing models. The opportunity to learn from more senior graduate students was a unique experience in this setup. There was a continuous exploration and application of theories and methodologies to agricultural problems.

From the point of view of development of the science of agricultural economics in India, the above points were beneficial. One major limitation of empirical analysis in Indian agriculture economics research has been the lack of computer facilities for large-scale and frequent data analysis. This is more so at the level of agricultural colleges and universities. For simple applications or analysis, this of course would not be a major constraint. The difficulty, however, is obvious from the fact that much empirical research in agricultural economics has taken place in institutions with in-house computer facilities. For expansion of empirical research it is necessary to make extensive computer facilities available to the researchers, at least at the university level. With the advent of micro-processors and statistical/ econometric software, this does not appear to be difficult to achieve.

The research infrastructure for inter- or multidisciplinary work has already been a feature of agricultural universities. However, strengthening economics and statistics programs through interaction with economists and statisticians outside the system would be considered advantageous.

The importance of training in agriculture for an agricultural economist has been discussed at length since the early years of the development of agricultural economics. So has the subject of having "modern" tools at the agricultural economists' disposal during this training. But the benefit of providing a varied learning atmosphere to the students by having students of different regions, backgrounds, and training backgrounds has not been adequately understood. This is an aspect that needs to be examined further in India — which offers so much variety within the country — and could provide an additional impetus to the development of agricultural economics research in the country.

REFERENCES

Askari, H., and J. T. Cummings. 1976. *Agricultural Supply Response: A Survey of the Econometric Evidence.* New York: Praeger Publishers.

Bhagwati, J. N., and S. Chakravorty. 1971. *Contributions to Indian Economic Analysis: A Survey.* New Delhi: Lalvani Publishing House.

Desai, D. K. 1960. Linear Programming Applied to Problems in Indian Agriculture. *Indian Journal of Agricultural Economics,* 15(2):59–65.

Dey, A. K., and A. Rudra. 1973. A Test of Hypothesis of Rational Allocation under Cobb-Douglas Technology. *Economic and Political Weekly,* 8(24).

Heady, E. O. 1946. Production Functions for a Random Sample of Farms. *Journal of Farm Economics,* 28(4):989–1104.

Heady, E. O. 1952a. Use and Estimation of Input-Output Relationships or Productivity Coefficients. *Journal of Farm Economics,* 34:115–127.

Heady, E. O. 1952b. *Economics of Agricultural Production and Resources Use.* New York: Prentice Hall.

Heady, E. O., and S. Bhide (eds.). 1983. *Livestock Response Functions*. Ames: Iowa State
    University Press.
Heady, E. O., and W. Candler. 1958. *Linear Programming Methods*. Ames: Iowa State
    University Press.
Heady, E. O., and J. L. Dillon. 1961. *Agricultural Production Functions*. Ames: Iowa
    State University Press.
Hexem, R., and E. O. Heady. 1978. *Water Production Functions in Irrigated Agriculture*.
    Ames: Iowa State University Press.
Hopper, D. W. 1965. Allocation Efficiency in a Traditional Indian Agriculture. *Journal
    of Farm Economics*, 47:263–278.
Jacob, T., V. N. Amble, M. L. Mathur, and A. Subba Rao. 1969. Milk Production
    Functions and Optimum Feeding Schedules. *Indian Journal of Agricultural Econom-
    ics*, 24(2):35–44.
Jai Krishna. 1961. A Linear Programming Model for the Selection of Crop Enter-
    prises on an Average Farm in Western Ottar Pradesh. *Indian Journal of Agricultural
    Economics*, 16(4):13–21.
Raj Krishna. 1964. Some Production Functions for the Punjab. *Indian Journal of
    Agricultural Economics*, 19(3–4):87–97.
Randhawa, N. S., and E. O. Heady. 1966. Spatial Programming of Production for
    Agricultural Development in India. *Indian Journal of Agricultural Economics*,
    21(3):14–22.
Sen, S. R. 1959. Agricultural Economics Research and Economic Planning in India.
    Indian Journal of Agricultural Economics, 14(4):66–72.

V. NAZARENKO

11

Soviet Research into the Use of Economical and Mathematical Methods in Agriculture

I n recent decades econometrics has been increasingly important in the development of modern economics. Research work being carried on in many countries, including both the United States and the former USSR, is marked by quantitative changes in modern methods of statistical analysis and by the extensive use of mathematical approaches in economic research. The use of econometrics perhaps came later in agricultural science than in other disciplines because of both less-developed databases and methods of analyses. But we have long been aware of an imperative need for an intensive use of econometrics in agriculture. Originally, this trend manifested itself in the more extensive use of methods of statistical analysis. Methods and approaches used in the late 1950s and early 1960s now seem very simple, but they were important attempts to employ mathematic approaches in agriculture. I would like to emphasize that from the very beginning, econometric methods have been of scientific, theoretical,

V. Nazarenko is a policy official in Russia.

and applied importance to agriculture.

Linear programming methods were to a considerable extent elaborated as far back as during the prewar period in the USSR, and during the postwar period they were being introduced into economic research along with conventional methods of statistical analyses. In the Soviet Union, their application was confined to the industrial sphere. In the United States these methods were used to a greater extent in the sphere of merely statistical research.

Heady was the first, perhaps, to practice more extensive application of these methods in agriculture. His first publications in the 1950s were devoted to the optimization of agricultural production processes; problems which had been a traditional subject of economic research, such as rational use of production factors and maximizing the efficiency or resource use, were approached using linear programming methods. Not only did these publications acquire special scientific and theoretical importance, but they enjoyed extensive practical use in elaborating rational rates of fertilizer application, in manufacturing formulated feedstuffs, and in optimizing the cropping pattern.

Heady's work became known in the Soviet Union in the late 1950s. In the mid-1960s Heady was invited to Moscow to deliver lectures on the possibilities of using methods of econometric analysis in Soviet agriculture. According to Heady, the studies of methods and sources of statistical information in the Soviet Union were very fruitful. The Soviet Union has a huge corpus of statistical data in the form of state and collective farm reports. Heady mentioned that so much available statistical information provided possibilities for using econometrics extensively and for obtaining considerable and reliable information/analytic data for use at research institutions and relevant state departments.

We displayed a keen interest in Heady's works. Two books by Earl Heady had been translated into Russian; one dealt with problems related to linear programming methods, the other was on production functions. These books in the Russian language helped familiarize large numbers of Soviet economists with Heady's research methods.

Rapid development of econometric research in Soviet agricultural economics had commenced. Originally, the Department of Econometrics was established at the Research Institute for Agricultural Economics, then econometrics was dealt with in a group of departments, and in 1969 the All-Union Research Institute of Cybernetics in Agriculture was established to introduce econometric research in agriculture.

I recall my personal meetings with Heady first during my stay at Iowa State University in 1959 and then at the International Conference of Agricultural Economists in Mexico in 1961. Personal contacts with Heady helped to organize advanced training courses for several young Soviet economists at Iowa State University. Our relations with Iowa State University have never ceased. We regularly exchange scientific information. To a certain extent research work carried on by Heady ran parallel to that conducted in the Soviet Union—from initial building of rather simple linear programming models, calculations of production functions, and functional analysis to the development of complex regional and national simulation models for both the United States and the USSR.

The research work was conducted based on specific objectives we were to achieve with all the differences between the Soviet and U.S. economies, with adapted information and database systems, naturally, taken into account. I believe that under these conditions mutual exchange of information and ideas existed for the benefit of both countries. Contacts with Iowa State University have been maintained since 1973 in conformity with an agricultural agreement between the Soviet Union and the United States. A number of Soviet delegations have visited Iowa State University, and I recall my last visit in 1979.

Another contact maintained with Heady relates to the International Institute of Applied Systems Analysis (IIASA) in Vienna. Program research work on food and agriculture conducted at this institute and the methods used were very close to those employed both by Professor Heady and our researchers. The principal objective was to use methods of simulation modeling to build regional and national models and then a world food model.

Heady, as one of the most outstanding modeling specialists in the world, has undoubtedly greatly influenced the trends in research work being conducted at IIASA. IIASA shall participate not only in developing the world food model but also in carrying out parallel experiments aimed at building two regional models—one for Iowa

State and the other for the Stavropol territory. The principal objective of this research is to establish the effect of technology changes on the economic characteristics of agricultural production as well as ecological consequences resulting from changes in agricultural production and various forms of its intensification. Analytical research work is to be conducted in other countries. IIASA will publish a book summarizing to a certain extent the results of these experiments in the hope that they will become available to a broad circle of researchers. We would like to believe that the above-mentioned experiments will be conducted in conformity with those being carried out by the group of our researchers and those researchers at Iowa State University.

Soviet scientists have long held Heady and his scientific works in high esteem. Taking into account his great merits as a scientist, the All-Union Academy of Agricultural Sciences elected him its foreign member in 1984. Election to the position of Academy member is regarded as deep appreciation of one's scientific achievements. Heady is the only foreign member of our Academy.

We hope that Iowa State University will continue to actively cooperate with our Soviet economists in the development of a number of methodological aspects of research in the tradition of cooperation established with Heady and his disciples as well as with the Center for Agriculture and Rural Development. We believe that Heady's disciples will not only continue his research but will retain his sincerity and goodwill as well as his comprehensive approach to the problems of world cooperation.

KEITH D. ROGERS

12

B31

Impact on a Nation: The Professor, the Students, and the Institutions

Earl Heady

This chapter highlights one part of the work and contributions of Dr. Earl O. Heady in an international context. The work in, for, and with Thailand exemplifies the contact and impact he had on individuals, nations, and international regions. With little question, the "Heady shop" has had a greater impact on agricultural policy and planning in Thailand than in any other country, possibly including the United States. Heady's work in Thailand represents the true extension of a man, his philosophy and commitment to excellence, and the growth of the science through the teaching and impact of his students.

The work in Thailand is truly the story of a professor and his students, and the legacy that they have left a nation and on international region. Of course, the key student in this case was a young Thai professional from the Ministry of Agriculture and Cooperatives (MOAC) in Thailand. Somnuk Sriplung came to Iowa State University to study quantitative methods of economic analysis with Heady. Little could this student know when he was learning to do economic

Keith D. Rogers is Dean, College of Agriculture,
Arkansas State University, State University, Arkansas.

and statistical analysis with the assistance of manual Monroe calculators in the Statistics Lab that he would return to Thailand to lead a
team of Thai and U.S. professionals that would design and construct
numerous national, regional, and farm-level computer models as the
basis of agricultural sector analysis.

Internationalization is one of the buzz words today on campuses
and in government agencies around the world. The Thai connection,
as it has come to be affectionately named by many, represents a high
degree of integration and bonding of science and culture. The out-
ward manifestation of the work in Thailand was a series of activities
which have loosely been referred to as model building. In fact, the
projects represented the institutionalization of a basic philosophy that
the application of economic principles and quantitative analysis could
be effectively used to address real problems and provide carefully
considered alternative solutions in developing nations, as well as in
developed nations. Heady was determined to demonstrate that improved analytical capability would allow for more efficient allocation
of limited resources (private and public) to solve economic and social
problems in the agricultural sector with significant beneficial impact
for the rest of the economy.

Thailand was an experiment in one sense. Heady and Somnuk
believed that the progress that had been made over several decades in
quantitative analysis in the United States could be transferred, applied, and institutionalized in Thailand in a relatively short period of
time. Not only was the hypothesis correct, but the bonding of individuals that developed during the process transcends any project, unit of
government, or institution. The graduate training and subsequent
projects that were undertaken merged the careers and personal lives
of a large number of Thai and American professionals and families.
Those linkages today reach far beyond the Office of Agricultural
Economics (OAE) in Bangkok and Iowa State University (ISU) in
Ames.

While mathematical and conceptual models were a vehicle, the
projects were far more than an exercise in modeling. In fact, Heady
clearly viewed the work in Thailand as an effort to build personal and
institutional capacities to use all available resources, including linkages to other professionals in the world, to more effectively communicate the appropriate choices and consequences of critical policy and

resource allocation decisions at all levels of public and private decision-making. Those linkages are manifested in a cadre of some 200 or
more professionals in MOAC who worked directly on components of
the projects and another 200–300 staff members who worked in direct
support of the staff assigned to the projects. That cadre is linked in
self-sustaining informal relationships to professionals in government
agencies and universities around the world, and the linkages continue
to grow with their own energy.

The international bonding started with Heady bringing students
from around the world together in Ames, including representatives
from both the free world and from planned economies. That "melting
pot" provided a fertile environment for development of high standards
of quantitative analysis and scientific inquiry but also provided an
internationalization of the graduate program that created a sensitivity
and compassion for shared knowledge and experiences. The environment built the kind of lasting personal and professional relationships
that have allowed Heady's students to share a common bonding
around the world—bonding that forms a solid basis for sharing of
expertise, the value of which can never be quantified.

Two projects have provided the formal basis for much of the
graduate training and the assignment of long-term and short-term
specialists to work in Thailand. Both projects were cooperative agree-
ments between the Royal Thai Government (RTG) and the United
States Agency for International Development (AID/Thailand) in the
form of project grants to ISU for technical assistance to the MOAC
through the Division of Agricultural Economics (DAE), which was
upgraded in August of 1979 to the Office of Agricultural Economics.

The joint projects were developed in response to a direct requests by the MOAC for cooperation and collaboration in the development and application of sector analysis methods and models that
could be operated and maintained by the staff in OAE to develop
practical recommendations for the future development of Thailand's
agricultural sector at national, regional, and local levels. The first
project, Agricultural Sector Analysis (ASAP), was initiated on July 1,
1973, and continued through June 1979. The second project, Agricultural Planning (APP), was initiated on July 1, 1982, and continued through October 1985. The major ISU project team for ASAP
was in Thailand for five years, with one person remaining a sixth

year to provide miscellaneous assistance and coordination for maintenance and support of the models and databases that had been developed. The ISU project team was in Thailand a little over three years
to support the APP. The OAE staff demonstrated repeatedly, before
and after the departure of the ISU teams, that they had achieved the
capacity to apply improved data collection methodology, to conduct
quantitative economic analysis, and to formulate meaningful agricultural policy designed to address problems facing the Kingdom.

Several USAID personnel were involved in the initiative to implement agricultural sector analysis projects around the world, but
Heady cited Art Coutu for playing a critical role in facilitating the
extension of agricultural sector analysis to developing areas as program leader in agricultural sector analysis for USAID/Washington.
In Thailand, Fletcher E. Riggs played a critical role in inspiring and
supporting the projects as director for agricultural development for
USAID/Thailand. Other USAID personnel played important roles
in establishing and supporting the projects. Sriplung, director of the
DAE, served as project director for both projects for MOAC. Heady
served as project leader for the ASAP for Iowa State, and this author
served as the project leader for the APP for Iowa State. Personnel
serving long-term assignments on the teams in Thailand also included
Arthur J. Stoecker, Kenneth J. Nicol, J. Edwin Faris, Dan C.
Tucker, Leroy Blakeslee, Dennis M. Conley, Charles F. Framingham,
James A. Stephenson, Larry Kinyon, Herbert F. Fullerton, O. Neal
Walker, Wayne D. Ellingson, Gary Vocke, and Winton Fuglie. The
first five listed above provided leadership as chief-of-party of the ISU
teams in Thailand.

THE FIRST PROJECT

As cited at various places in the project literature, Agricultural
Sector Analysis in Thailand evolved from a strong desire by the
MOAC and other RTG agencies to deal more forcefully and efficiently with basic problems facing the agricultural sector and its integration into the national economy. After extensive discussions with
Heady, RTG, and USAID, the mutual recommendation was to expand cooperation between USAID and RTG with the purpose of

establishing an operational and self-sustaining agricultural sector analysis capability and plan implementation system within MOAC. The project was to develop the capability of MOAC to construct and use a complex of large-scale computerized econometric models, including a national linear programming model of Thai agriculture based on zonal and regional models, demand analysis models for Thai agricultural products, transportation and marketing models for major Thai commodities, regional development models, and a macro model linking the national linear programming model to selected segments of the nonagricultural sectors.

The project researchers were directly concerned with the 25 million people living in rural households in Thailand. In 1976 these people made up 58.4 percent of the nation's population. The net income from farm and nonfarm sources averaged only 9,000 baht (US$450) per household, or only 1,540 baht ($77) per capita for these rural residents.

The RTG was attempting to develop policies and programs to increase employment opportunities in the rural areas and reduce the discrepancies in rural-urban income equity, while providing for expanded food production to meet projected domestic consumption goals and simultaneously maintaining or expanding export levels. Decision-makers faced the complex problems of choosing and allocating the scarce government resources (personnel and capital) among competing policy or program alternatives with widely varying impacts on the short- and long-run development of the Thai economy. Raising income level of the poorest segment of the economy merited immediate attention, but extreme care had to be exercised to identify and develop alternatives that are complementary to, rather than competitive with, the ongoing economic growth. A misallocation of scarce Thai resources could have resulted in even lower relative income levels for the poor rural majority.

As cited in *Agricultural Development Planning in Thailand* (1982, p. x), several characteristics made the DAE/ISU agricultural sector analysis effort unique:

> 1. Several facets of the sector analysis program were initiated in a relatively short time even with the initial absence of a data processing mechanism, basic data bank, and trained Thai personnel. Regional and

national programming models reflecting special competition were operational approximately two years after full initiation of the project. A version of the macro model also was completed in two years after arrival of the macroeconomist on the ISU team. These are rather rapid accomplishments, considering the nature and availability of the data; the void in trained and experienced manpower; and the necessity to divert a large number of the ISU personnel to the on-the-job training program, research advisory activities, and policy analysis support for the DAE.

2. The project personnel emphasized a complete meshing and integration of ISU and Thai staffs in the development and implementation of the models and policy analysis conducted within this model framework. This accomplishment was made possible through common working conditions and complete interpersonal trust between DAE and ISU staff members, which was built through the intensive person-to-person training and research approach established by DAE leaders as the means to implement integration of ISU and DAE staffs.

3. Within the capabilities of their training, the DAE staff has been able to comprehend the model developments and applications. They are capable and have independently formulated policy questions and conducted the analysis utilizing the analytical systems developed.

4. The major models have been applied to the real world and important Thai policy problems. Thai administrators and institutions are acquainted with availability of the models for policy analysis and with the purposes for which they are designed. However, accomplishments are small relative to the possibilities posed for the future. The present models are being expanded and updated, but presently they can facilitate a wide range of policy analysis on the future of the agricultural sector, and plans exist for the implementation of a range of policy studies. These possibilities now exist with the maturation of the models to their present status and the return of many of the DAE senior staff from graduate training programs.

5. The models are detailed and can relate economic impacts back to the zone level. They contrast to others that can generate results only at national levels. The Thai models are directed to answer not only "what" at the national level, but also "where" and "by how much" at the zone level. Extensions of specifications to changwats (provinces) and typical farms will ultimately provide this analytical capability to the changwat governor's staff for local analysis.

6. The accomplishments of this project have been recognized by other less developed countries of Southeast Asia, which have suggested that an agricultural sector analysis center be established at the DAE in Bangkok to catalyze similar developments in other countries of the region.

Policymakers and researchers in Thailand faced basically the same issues and problems that are faced in all countries, including developed economies, but in many cases the database and the analytical capability was inadequate to fully integrate key components of comprehensive policy recommendations to enhance the growth and development of the agriculture sector and the national economy. Thailand was concerned about growth in income and employment and about reducing income and employment disparities between the rural and urban people, among regions, and between the agricultural sector and the rest of the Kingdom. Thailand was also concerned with expanding the potential for increasing agricultural production to ensure adequate food supplies and to earn foreign exchange. Discussions of import substitution and export expansion in the agricultural sector surface often in the context of discussions of gross national product, population, and export earnings. Rapid expansion of domestic demand as a result of the increasing population has slowly eroded these important sources of foreign exchange and reduced per capita productivity in the sector. Most of the growth in agricultural productivity in Thailand has been through land-extensive methods, which cannot be relied upon in the future as the government will have to act to protect its environment from excessive land conversion.

Because of the unique location of the country and the dominance of the agricultural sector in a large portion of Thailand, the nation faces some rather unique political and economic challenges in large portions of the rural sector where poverty is common and unrest has the opportunity to expand. There was sufficient motivation among farmers and government policymakers to explore the potential of expanding irrigation, to push for higher participation in multiple cropping systems, and to utilize improved farming technologies. Seasonal unemployment and underemployment are wide spread in the agricultural sector. Like many other developing economies, Thailand suffers from a high rate of immigration from low-income rural areas into the urban centers (primarily Bangkok), which accentuates problems of congestion and unemployment in the nonagricultural sectors.

As cited in *Agricultural Development Planning in Thailand* (1982), there was no scarcity of issues and problems to provide a focus for DAE research and program development. Those with some chance to be addressed within the limit of DAE facilities included (1) price and income response for major agricultural commodities, including demand analysis and commodity supply responses; (2) land and irrigation expansion potentials and alternative methods for increasing per rai (2.5 rai = 1.0 acre) and per capita productivity (new varieties, fertilizer, management); (3) investment in expanded agricultural research and educational programs for relevant crops in the various zones; (4) analysis of fertilizer use alternatives for rice and upland crops; (5) resource utilization, including capital for labor substitution, especially in the power category; (6) agricultural marketing and transportation; (7) distribution impacts of national programs on agriculture and of agriculture on the national economy; and (8) relationships between retail prices of selected food crops, foreign exchange earnings, and farm income.

As an overview, there are many elements that could be identified as contributing significantly to the success of the two agricultural sector projects in Thailand. Obviously, the environment and the overall design had to be appropriate. Funding and qualified personnel had to be available and at adequate levels to support and sustain the effort. There had to be institutional commitments on the part of all parties to support and nurture the projects. These were all put in place through the efforts of the individuals cited earlier.

Heady pointed to the operational approach of the team effort many times as the most significant factor in the success of agricultural sector planning in Thailand. As he had done in Ames, he insisted on achieving effective communication and interaction among the researchers and between researchers and policymakers. Sriplung subscribed to the basic approach so strongly that he arranged for a retreat to the north of Thailand for key members of his staff that would be working on the ASAP and the ISU team within a few days of the team's arrival in Thailand. The retreat included time for visitation to ongoing DAE research and demonstration projects throughout the Central Plains and North, intensive discussions of research priorities and tentative timetables, and time for Thai staff to show the "farangs" some of the finer points of entertainment and relaxation. Without a doubt, the week of study, planning, and bonding was the single most significant factor in explaining the close collaborative relationships that were developed between the Thai staff and ISU team members. Followed by a proven intent for the ISU team to work with the Thai staff for their growth and development, the rapport that was initiated on the retreat expanded through close cooperation. The transfer from one team member to another was critical in bridging differences in cultural and professional backgrounds of the Thai staff and the ISU team members.

Several principles were established to guide the cooperative effort:

1. The ISU team members were to conduct research with, and not for, the Thai team members. The intent was to fully institutionalize the analytical capability with the Thai staff from the first data collection so that the Thai researchers would be able to bring their full knowledge of the Thai environment to the process at every step and guarantee that the models were not abstractions that would later prove inappropriate and render them unreliable.

2. The selection of alternative modeling techniques and concepts was specifically conditioned by their compatibility with the skills and training of the Thai staff and the ease with which that expertise was learned, applied, and transferred. Researchers cannot be expected to correctly apply models and methodology which they do not fully understand.

3. Every effort was made to ensure that the Thai researchers understood what they were doing as the model construction and analysis progressed so that they would understand why each component was important, and so that each component could be reproduced after departure of the ISU team.

4. ISU team members had their offices in the MOAC with the Thai staff, and hence the Thai staff and ISU team members all shared the same work environment. This working environment was a critical factor in maintaining the openness and continuous interaction of the Thai staff and ISU team. The environment provided the ISU team with firsthand insights and exposure to information and issues confronting the Thai staff.

5. Research models, methods, and priorities were considered and established jointly. The joint process insured that the priorities, assumptions, methods, data needs, and other constraints were consistent with the experience of the Thai staff. Insights of the Thai staff were critical in making assessments of practical limitations to the

database, models, analysis, and policy options.

6. The ultimate goal of the ISU team was to make their roles redundant. Each project had a fixed term, and the overriding objective was to develop the skill and knowledge of the Thai staff to duplicate the expertise of the ISU team members and for the Thai staff to assume full responsibility for every component of the project as quickly as possible. This was facilitated to a great extent by having a Thai staff member assigned to serve as project leader for each component of the project.

The principles that were developed to guide the relationships between the research team and the government policymakers were equally important in developing and maintaining relationships that provided for free flow of ideas and feedback to the analytical work. While most of the concepts are equally appropriate for researchers in any setting, the set of guidelines proved to be very valuable in the Thai setting since the government changed several times during the course of the projects. These principles included the following concepts:

1. *Maintain an apolitical posture and a low profile.* Maintaining an apolitical posture is not easy during a time of political turmoil and perceived opportunity to fill a relative vacuum, but it is critical to be able to maintain confidence and trust to span more than one political group. This became very vivid as the government changed several times.

2. *Assist those actors to whom you relate in filling their roles and satisfying their needs.* The purpose of the project was to build an analytical capability to respond quickly to timely questions. The production and release of early information brought heavy demands for more information. The project and Thai staff were under constant pressure to allocate resources between building additional capability and using existing capability to respond to immediate requests for information.

3. *Involve civil service executives, technical-professional, and operating staff in your research.* The broader the base of technical staff involved in designing the research, the more likely it will be to address the most critical issues and the broader the base of confidence in the research.

4. *Respond to government requests for assistance.* This principle was

simply a reminder that the sole purpose of building the analytical capability in MOAC was to enhance the capacity to provide the appropriate information in a timely manner for use of political decision-makers.

5. *Do not promise things you cannot deliver.* It was very obvious in Thailand that it is easy to oversell the speed and capability with which reliable research can be accomplished. While it is sometimes distasteful to indicate that specific results cannot be produced with the existing capability, or can not be produced in a timely manner, it is far more damaging in the long run to create false expectations that cannot be fulfilled.

6. *Use carefully constructed models with a sound theoretical basis, the best available data, and sound statistical procedures.* These are the tools that other professionals and academics can review for accuracy and that help to minimize the chance for error of fact, omission, or interpretation.

7. *Know the quality of your results and be perfectly candid about it.* Economics is not like the physical sciences and often does not lend itself to precise measurement. Quantitative results may have high standard errors or only indicate order of magnitude and direction of change. It is essential to be candid about the statistical properties of all results that are released for use by the public decision-makers or other researchers.

8. *Present your results in a manner that can be readily understood by the lay person.* Many political decision-makers do not have the benefit of technical training in all disciplines, and they may have limited knowledge of the technical basis or language used in some research. They have limited time to read and interpret information. The quickest way to communicate is in lay terms that are easily understood and interpreted.

9. *Structure research capacity development so that useful results are produced at various stages.* This principle has solid basis in more than one area. First, this will no doubt lead one to develop models, databases, reports, and other output in ascending stages. This allows for useful information to be produced in a shorter period of time, and thus begin to satisfy the expectations of policymakers and others dependent upon the results. Especially with young and inexperienced researchers, including the ISU team as relating to the Thai economy, it

is critical to build relatively simple analytical methodology that can be verified for accuracy and consistency before proceeding to more sophisticated methodology and models.

10. *Make explicit all assumptions that are employed and their implications for interpretation and use of results.* Policymakers almost always have a set of restraints within which they feel they must operate. They must know the basic assumptions or constraints on which the analysis is constructed.

11. *Give others the spotlight.* This principle is always appropriate in helping to build working relationships with others, but it was especially important with an outside element such as the ISU team. It was critical to remember that the team was there to help the Thai staff provide analytical results and not to influence Thai policy or gain recognition for themselves.

12. *Be realistic.* Like economics itself, policymaking is something less than a precise science. Not all political decisions are made on the basis of pure economic implications. Thus, the best economic research may not be used in total or even in part at any given time. The test of progress is whether the policymakers consider the results, continue to solicit assistance, and tend to rely more heavily on the research results over time.

In addressing factors that contributed to the successful implementation of the ASAP, and the subsequent APP, it is critical not to overlook the strength of the DAE that existed prior to the arrival of the ISU teams. Readers are reminded that the ASAP was recommended to strengthen an existing capacity for data collection, analysis, and policy formulation. DAE already had a relatively large staff at the central office in Bangkok and additional field staff located at various research and administrative centers around the country. Procedures were in place for data collection, processing, and reporting. Leadership was provided by Sriplung and a small cadre of staff members who had received master's degrees or had had other advanced study in various academic institutions outside of Thailand.

Prior to the arrival of the ISU teams, the DAE staff undertook a comprehensive investigation of the regional characteristics of Thailand's agricultural sector. The results were used to identify 19 unique agroeconomic zones to be used as basic regional planning units for agricultural development and commodity programs. The statistical branch of DAE had carried out a comprehensive cross-sectional survey of the rural farm sector. The data from the initial survey provided a basis for characterizing resource use, identifying production possibilities, and establishing base input and technology levels in each planning zone. Subsequent surveys were designed and conducted to supplement the cross-sectional data from the 1971–1972 survey.

The agroeconomic planning zones were identified along boundary lines of contiguous political units to facilitate later implementation of specific policies on a local level. The zones were differentiated to the maximum extent possible based on similar soil types, rainfall level and seasonal distribution, temperature patterns and fluctuations, type of farming units present, level of technology, income level, communication and transportation patterns, and other characteristics that would tend to create a natural regional unit.

The overall operational plan developed for the ASAP during the staff and administrative retreat to the North was to construct a national interregional competition linear programming model of the agricultural sector in Thailand. Other analytical and modeling efforts would be developed to support and extend the national model. As indicated earlier, the strategy was to work with units that the staff could identify with and to use practical knowledge to guide model construction and interpretation of preliminary results for accuracy and reliability. The strategy that was implemented involved construction of 19 stand-alone zone models with consistent and compatible structure that could be integrated into four regional models (Central Plains, North, Northeast, and South), and later into one national interregional competition model.

There are many ways to teach linear programming and model construction, and many may view it as a highly mathematical and technical process. In understanding the process and source of intense rapport that was built between the Thai staff and the ISU team at this time, it is helpful to sophisticated quantitative researchers operating in isolated "think tanks" on high-speed mainframes to visualize the job at hand. The ISU staff had to develop confidence in the knowledge of the Thai staff about the production conditions and technology, and the Thai staff had to develop confidence in the ISU team's ability to build a computer model when DAE did not even have a computer or any staff trained in the appropriate computer skills. The first zone model was initially constructed in total on a huge paper mat that covered the conference table and quickly spilled over onto the open area in the middle of the floor in the administrative office. Many sessions were conducted on the floor around this huge mat with Thai and U.S. staff from doctorate level to clerks side by side discussing the meaning and purpose of every coefficient entered in that initial matrix. Toss in cultural shyness, language barriers, and translators (both technical and linguistics), and you have the basis for the team concept and mutual trust that evolved and became the dominant strength of the DAE/ISU relationship.

Within a few weeks DAE's computer arrived, was tested and installed, and the process of getting the model(s) on the computer began. From those modest beginnings evolved a core of Thai staff that understood the basic concepts of constructing a linear programming model, and they provided the leadership in designing and constructing the other 18 zone models in close collaboration with the ISU team.

The initial models were crop-based production models with livestock activities and related demand as exogenous adjustments to the model. Crop-livestock interfaces were introduced at a later date in the regional and national models. Interregional demand and transportation activities were represented by exogenous constraints in the zone models and were added as activities in the regional and national models.

Need to provide input and provide support for development of the Fourth Five-Year Plan for agriculture provided focus for the DAE/ISU team and created a real urgency and demand for a reliable product. The ultimate test of capability came in late 1975 when the National Economic and Social Development Board (NESDB) requested that DAE develop the five-year plan and supporting documentation. A set of policy objectives were identified in consultation with NESDB staff, government representatives, politically appointed officials, and influential citizens. Those objectives included (1) raising the level of income in Thailand and improving its distribution to farm and nonfarm people, (2) increasing employment opportunities, (3) producing adequate food supplies for all Thai people at reasonable prices, (4) improving national security and unity, (5) increasing the level of foreign exchange earnings, and (6) providing for the right of individual farmers to own land. These objectives became the basis for analysis and assessment of components of the five-year plan.

Based on aggregate demand and supply factors, three principal plan alternatives were specified and four complementary illustrations were outlined. The national model was used to evaluate each of the three principal plan alternatives and four complementary alternatives under three different assumptions concerning growth of population, consumption, and exports. Detailed assessments of each of the plan objectives were summarized and presented for review. These detailed documents and rationale for development of the assumptions became the basis for formulation of the Fourth Five-Year Plan for agriculture.

Within a limited resource environment, trade-offs become essential in resource allocation. The capacity and speed of the IBM 1130 computer in DAE was a significant constraint. With the magnitude of training assignments that reduced available Thai staff in the short run, and the magnitude of activities initiated by DAE in response to emerging analytical capacity, staff time also became a critical constraint. Given the regional nature of many of the government programs, it was appropriate to utilize the smaller regional models for more detailed analysis of specific problems. As indicated earlier, regional models were developed for each of the four geographic regions, starting with the Northeast. The regional models were utilized to conduct a series of studies assessing supply response, employment, and productivity.

The regional models were designed to focus on income and employment alternatives in specific regions. The supply studies were normative in nature and focused on a set of specific dominant crops in each region. Specifically, the models were designed to estimate supply response for selected crops under a wide range of assumed prices, and to measure the impact on resource use, production patterns of other commodities, employment, and income potential. Each of the regional models retained the zone model and activity identity so that the potential impacts could be traced to specific planning units. While the regional models were normative in nature and no direct empirical evidence was presented to guarantee that farmers would respond as indicated, there is strong evidence in Thailand that farmers do respond to economic incentives.

In an economy where draft animals were used as a primary power source for tillage and cultivation, the decline in bovine population became a policy issue. An independent national bovine model was developed to analyze the trends in bovine population as a source of power and meat. Subsequently, the bovine model was integrated into the national crop model to reflect the complementary and competitive nature of crop and livestock production in this environment. The addition of the bovine model provided for endogenous estimates of impact on crop production, draft animal power, and meat supply.

A fourth set of research activities and models dealt with commodity markets in Thailand. Unlike the linear programming models that were used for the bulk of the crop and livestock modeling, the commodity models were "stand-alone" models. The commodity models were constructed as a set of simultaneous equations used to represent the operation of specific important variables in real-world markets. Two types of equations were used. Behavioral equations were used to model distinct groups of agents in the market. Identity equations were used to specify equilibrium conditions and other known relations of an exact nature.

A fifth set of research activities involved specification of macroeconomic models to evaluate key exogenous factors and interactions between the agricultural sector and other sectors of the Thai economy. Unlike the LP models, the macroeconomic models were primarily based on time series regression analysis. Full linkage to integrate the LP models and the macroeconomic model would have been extremely difficult because the models are based on two very different techniques and DAE was operating under severely limited computer capacity. Thus, the macroeconomic models were developed as stand-alone models to be used recursively in conjunction with the LP models for assessment of interactions with the agricultural sector. Two basic structures were developed. The first model was linear in both parameters and variables, while the second was linear in parameters but nonlinear in variables.

A sixth set of research activities and models were focused on demographic changes and migration. These models were designed to account for independent growth and geographic movement of disaggregated segments of the population. The primary demand for the demography data arises from requirements for both the agricultural production models and the macroeconomic models. Aggregated data was available for key census years but not for specific planning years or on a disaggregated basis. Disaggregation by sex and age are important in projecting population growth and migration. The demography models were designed to provide more accurate estimates of projected regional population to improve the accuracy of demand and labor force coefficients in the agricultural sector planning models.

A seventh set of research and model-building activities addressed transportation, storage, and processing capacity. The primary objectives of these activities were to (1) characterize marketing patterns and trade flows by commodity, (2) develop unit costs and capacity by mode of transportation, (3) develop unit costs and capacity by location and type of storage, and (4) collect data on unit costs, through capacity, and conversion factors for processing under alternative types of technology and facilities. The transportation models were designed to provide the linkages between the zones and regions for interregional competition in the national LP models. The storage and processing models provided improved estimates of demand and capacity to handle increased volumes of commodities implied in the application of new technology and growth of the agricultural sector.

One last area of research activity and modeling involved recursive models for policy analysis. The primary focus of these planning models and research efforts was to pull together or link the agricultural sector parameters in the national LP models to the regional LP models and to the macroeconomic models. Because of the dominance of the agricultural sector in the Thai economy, it is critical that changes in that sector are effectively linked to the rest of the economy and concurrently reflect resulting changes in nonagricultural sectors. Examples of policy issues that might be considered in more detail after achieving a fuller linkage between the LP model(s) and the macroeconomic model include (1) the influence of export expansion and import substitution policies on farm income and balance of payments, (2) the effect of agricultural price policies on the cost of living, (3) the ability of the economy to provide employment for a growing population, (4) the effects of agricultural development policies on nonagricultural sectors and total economy, and (5) annual updates of the Five-Year Plan. Some of these key linkages are through farm income, agricultural employment, change in investment in agriculture and related industries, and change in purchase of inputs by agriculture from nonagricultural sectors.

In describing the research activities and modeling efforts which drew the most external attention, other components of the project should not be overlooked. As mentioned earlier, DAE established its own computer center during the ASAP project. DAE purchased and installed the hardware and software, developed operational procedures, trained personnel, developed internal capacity to provide programming support to other researchers, designed software to process survey data, and provided a wide range of data processing services. The heavy workload pushed the computer center to an around-the-clock schedule within a few months of installation. Down time for routine maintenance was only scheduled reluctantly and when absolutely necessary. Before DAE was authorized to staff a second and third shift for operation of the computer center, members of the ISU team and their Thai counterparts were forced to learn the basic system operation procedures and the binary system of error codes so they could take turns supervising the operation of the system after routine working hours in order to extend the time the system was in operation. With the speed and capacity of desktop computers that are available today, it is difficult to bring into focus the problems that were encountered when the first zone model took approximately 40 hours of actual computing time to solve. With two or three system interruptions and two scheduled halts in the computing process, delivery of that first labor of love took nearly a week of time after all of the coefficients were correctly loaded in the machine and the actual computing had been initiated. It has often been said that necessity is the mother of invention, but truer words could not have been spoken. Techniques were immediately designed and introduced to reduce the computing time and facilitate reoptimization.

Certainly, the ASAP project could not have produced the results it did without the excellent support of the Agricultural Statistics group. The existing database was fragmented in places and subject to normal errors, but it provided the primary base on which the modeling could be initiated and weaknesses in the database could be identified. In addition to responsibility for economic analysis, DAE had been given responsibility for data collection, processing, and reporting of agricultural statistics. Other units of MOAC also generated selected agricultural statistics through various reporting procedures. In some cases, multiple sets of conflicting data were in circulation, making analysis and planning an even more difficult assignment. Technical assistance was provided to DAE to assist in improving the data collection and processing procedures.

The entire focus of the ASAP was institution building — building indigenous capacity to conduct quantitative and qualitative research and to support the decision-making process in the RTG as it related to the agricultural sector and agricultural development. The close working relationship between the Thai staff and the ISU team facilitated extensive on-the-job training. The Thai staff was ready, eager, and determined to not only duplicate but learn the "how" and "why" of every aspect of the work that was produced in cooperation with the ISU team. Many of the Thai counterparts spent 8- to 12-hour days in intense discussion, planning, and research sessions conducted in English for the benefit of their "farang" friends, and then assembled again for independent or group study and discussion sessions. As a note, unless you have lived or worked in another culture, you may not fully appreciate the intense stress involved in trying to work — not just get around town — in a second language. The study sessions were to interpret what they had heard during the planning meetings or to study technical support material where they felt they were weak. These study sessions involved economic theory, statistical methods, mathematical modeling, basic computer programming, computer system operation, policy concepts, and all the other concepts associated with the research effort. Heady insisted that the ISU team make every effort to help the Thai staff understand each step of the process and joint effort. Sriplung sealed the technology transfer by demanding that the Thai staff be prepared at all times to explain to him or government officials outside DAE and MOAC what was being done, why, and what could be expected as results.

One of the problems faced on this project, and on any similar project, is the scheduling of formal graduate training if that opportunity is available. The ASAP contained a major training component that provided for six to eight doctorate programs and as many as twenty master's programs. The dilemma that Sriplung and the team had to face was that of choosing between short-run and long-run objectives. Selecting the most capable staff for graduate programs in the United States meant they would not be available to interact with the ISU team for all or most of the project. These individuals are, of course, the ones that would be expected to provide the most significant leadership in both the short run and the long run. Sriplung made the tough decisions, staggered the graduate training as much as possible, and provided for the long-term needs by making short-term sacrifices. This cadre of staff with advanced training, both before and during the ASAP, now provide the leadership in the program. This formal graduate training, and the practical training on the project, formed the bridge from Heady, through Sriplung and the ISU team, to the next generation of leaders in MOAC. They are now extending and expanding the linkages to a new mid-level management group that will be the leadership of tomorrow. Indeed, not only the capacity to conduct research was institutionalized, but also the capacity to develop new staff and management as the old "team" matures.

As one looks back on the team effort, the commitment of the Thai staff simply cannot be understated. These were, for the most part, permanent government officials who certainly did not receive any extra compensation for working 14-, 16-, and 18-hour days. Sriplung had simply instilled the search and demand for excellence in his staff that he had learned studying under Heady and refined in his own way. In perspective, there was adequate reinforcement in the system. The regular visits to the project and with the team by Heady left little doubt that he could always see how the team could have accomplished more with the available resources and time, and that he would expect that level of output by his next visit. Sriplung did not see a distinction between the ISU team and his own staff, so he also created and maintained high expectations for the ISU team. Sriplung clearly had learned his lessons very well. He extended those high levels of expectation to his staff, and they responded.

THE SECOND PROJECT

The second ISU project in Thailand was the Agricultural Planning Project (APP), and it was a direct outgrowth or extension of the ASAP. The primary purpose of the second project was to strengthen the capabilities of Thailand's Office of Agricultural Economics to carry out policy advisory responsibility, problem identification and analysis, planning, data management, and integrated project preparation functions. In 1979, DAE was promoted to the status of Office of Agricultural Economics (OAE). OAE was given substantially increased responsibility and authority for agricultural planning, policy analysis, budget analysis, and project preparation. DAE had grown substantially in personnel and budgets, and new increments of both were added with the upgrading to OAE status.

The APP was designed to help OAE strengthen its capacity and to improve performance by providing long-term technical assistance in its major functional areas. Short-term consultants, participant training, and procurement of selected equipment were provided in addition to the long-term technical assistance. Specific objectives set forth for the APP included:

1. To assist in developing a full range of managerial capabilities, with particular emphasis on coordinating and integrating OAE's resources to serve its new and expanded functions;

2. To assist in conceptualizing, designing, and installing ministry wide systems and procedures for development planning, policy analysis, and plan implementation (budgeting);

3. To provide system management support and, secondarily, specific policy advisory services;

4. To assist in developing institutional capability to manage data and information in such a way as to provide timely reporting and analysis of inputs for research, planning, and decision-making;

5. To assist in the development of institutional capability to systematically identify, design, monitor, and evaluate agricultural projects that address the objectives of national plans and policies;

6. To assist in developing proper sampling techniques to be used in collecting data on the economic conditions of farmers;

7. To provide advice and assistance over the full range of statistical responsibilities being undertaken by the OAE; and

8. To assist in developing a full range of computer utilization and data processing, data analysis and storage, computer training, and database systems for various agricultural subsections.

It is not difficult to follow the evolution of events in MOAC as they relate to the growth of OAE in stature and responsibility. The quality and scope of work produced by DAE created an ever-increasing demand for data, analysis of economic and social issues, and evaluation of policy alternatives. Four major areas were identified for long-term technical assistance. These included (1) planning and policy management, (2) project development and design, (3) economic and data analysis, and (4) agricultural statistics collection and management. Clearly, the emphasis of the second project represented a shift from technical assistance in economic research to technical assistance in economic research management.

One of the first assignments for the second ISU team was to assist in the review of the organizational structure of OAE and in the preparation of a recommendation for the reorganization and reallocation of resources to meet the new responsibilities. A comprehensive reorganization plan was developed that included reassignment of resources in the central offices in Bangkok and establishing area offices in each of the zones to provide increased capacity to respond to data collection through routine and special surveys and to facilitate closer linkages between local staff and the central office. Microcomputers were proposed for the area offices to perform standard data entry and error checking before electronic transmission to the central office through modems and telephone lines. The leap from no in-house computer capacity on the first project to microcomputers and electronic transfer of information on the second project in less than ten years may symbolize the rapid changes which were taking place in the working environment of OAE as much as any other example. New positions were identified, the civil service commission was petitioned for new slots and funding, researchers were promoted to new administrative positions, new personnel were hired and integrated into the system, productivity increased, and demand for output continued to grow.

The reorganization plan to decentralize OAE was approved and implementation was initiated to move a large number of employees, vehicles, and other pieces of equipment to the zone offices. The use of computer terminals, microcomputers, and commercial software packages was initiated to expedite data processing and to gain analytical proficiency in order to assist various divisions of OAE to provide better and more timely response to policy issues. SPSS-X software packages and training were purchased for both the mainframe and the microcomputers, as well as SUDS, MS-DOS, DBASE III (Thai/English version), Lotus 1-2-3 (Thai/English version), Thaistar, T-basic, EROS, and RIPS.

The economic and data analysis portion of the APP was designed to provide reduced, but continued, support for the modeling and data analysis activities initiated under the ASAP. The overall objective was to upgrade and extend the economic and data analysis research capability initiated under the ASAP and to assist in developing institutional capability to manage data and information in such a way as to provide timely reporting and analysis as an input for research planning and policy decision-making. Refinement and updating of coefficients in the models became a major activity. Part of the reorganization of OAE involved a reorientation of research units from a functional approach to a commodity approach. The need for a formal commodity situation reporting system was identified and the new system was designed and implemented. Finally, anticipation of needs to support the staff work to prepare for the Sixth Five-Year Plan became a priority focus for several research units.

While DAE had previously had some responsibility for project oversight and supervision, the responsibility was significantly increased with the new responsibilities for OAE. Technical assistance was scheduled to directly support development of a format for systematic review of projects, development of a system for monitoring and evaluating ongoing projects, and development of a summary reporting system for project budgets. Groundwater utilization was a current and pressing issue which became the central thrust for the project design work. A formal short course was organized and conducted for the staff on project identification, design, and preparation. Terminals and printers were rented with funds from the APP to provide a test of procedures for data entry and access to the project files. Terminals and microcomputers were purchased later to provide this access.

The primary objective of the agricultural statistics component of the APP was to help OAE and the Center for Agricultural Statistics improve the quality and timeliness of its official agricultural estimates for Thailand. Area frame sampling was identified as a methodology that would improve the overall survey methodology and was implemented as a part of the APP. New staff were hired on a temporary basis to assist with construction of the area sampling frames, selected maps and aerial photographs were ordered, and stratification and sample selection was completed one province at a time. Late in 1984, area survey frame was used to compare results with the list frame for the first time on a pilot basis. Significant improvements in accuracy were achieved with the new procedure. Objective yield survey methodology and use of Landsat satellite imagery were also introduced and tested. Considerable time and effort were devoted to establishing realistic timetables for data collection, processing, verification, and release that would meet scheduled and anticipated release dates for end users.

The final major area of assistance on the APP was for the computer system. As reflected in the rapid growth of the research workload in OAE, the pressure on the Computer Center for increased computing capacity and computing support raced out of sight. Technical assistance was provided to assist in developing specifications to upgrade the computer system, upgrade the programming skills of the staff through on-the-job training and formal instruction, and to assist in developing an efficient production control and computer center management system. While this technical assistance was designed as long-term assistance, USAID budget cuts forced a reduction in planned personnel and required that this assistance be provided through a series of short-term consultant assignments. Some of the most significant elements of upgrading the computing capacity in OAE included rental of four Sperry terminals to initiate interactive training and processing using Mapper software with the UNIVAC 110-60 mainframe that had been installed, procurement of five 256K Sperry microcomputers with hard-disk drives and letter-quality printers, procurement of a 64K Spectral Data RIPS Landsat microcomputer and data processing system with support training, procurement of 2400 baud modems to link the central office with the zone offices for data transmission, and procurement of the software packages that were mentioned earlier. Software and special processing programs were upgraded or redesigned to improve performance and serve special needs more effectively.

These comments are not intended to explain the detail of the work done with OAE, but rather to provide a general overview of the scope of activities that were undertaken by the ISU teams in Thailand. The attempt here is to provide some perspective of the range of activities and the large number of Thai staff that were involved over the life of the two projects. Certainly the cryptic notes have not done justice to the work of the long-term and short-term ISU team members who worked in Thailand over a 14-year period, nor have the brief comments done justice to the total contributions of the Thai staff during and following the ISU projects. The intent was only to give some feeling and appreciation for the points of contact that Heady had in the Thai system.

It has been my privilege and honor to share some of my thoughts and insights about some of the significant contributions that Heady made in Thailand through his own work and that of his Thai and American students. It has given me a chance to reflect on the impact that he has had upon agriculture and agricultural development in that nation. I have had the opportunity to return to Thailand in 1989 and 1991 to visit old friends inside and outside of MOAC. Leadership at OAE is now in the hands of the next generation, and the performance and responsibility of OAE continues to grow. The joint effort is as meaningful today as it was when the Thai staff and ISU team labored side by side to build those first models in 1973. The ISU luncheon last summer for "Khun" Keith and "Khun" Judy was no doubt a surrogate expression of pride and appreciation for the contributions made by Heady, his students, and the joint accomplishments of the DAE/ISU team.

The focus of my discussion has been on the contributions which Heady made as a scientist. Hidden in that discussion was more than one hint of compassion and personal impact. Within the context of this commemorative book, I think it is appropriate to focus some light on the person as well as the scientist par excellence. As indicated earlier, Heady maintained high expectations for the ISU team and for the Thai counterparts, and he was not bashful about pressing those expectations upon the team. However, there is another significant side to his contribution to the team in Thailand, a side which others will no doubt address in the context of work and support in other settings. Heady not only served as a forceful scientific team leader for the ISU team, but he went home with us at night to discuss family concerns and sat on the floor playing with our young children. This was a giant among men by all accounts, and yet he had the time and

sensitivity to serve as a father and grandfather figure for the young
ISU team members that were far from the security of their academic
institutions, families, and other support structures. Herein lies part of
the explanation for the motivation and strength he was able to impart
to Sriplung, the ISU team, many of the Thai staff members, and to
other young scientists around the world. We believed in the man as
well as the scientist.

I find myself with the same loss for words that I experienced
when I tried to put together a meaningful acknowledgement in my
dissertation. Again, I find myself drawn back to the same poem that
Judy and I found on the library shelves one night during a break
while studying for exams in the ISU library. The title is "The Bridge
Builder" and the author was listed as anonymous.

> An old man going a lone highway,
> Came, at the evening cold and gray,
> To a chasm vast and deep and wide.
> The old man crossed in the twilight dim,
> The sullen stream had no fear for him;
> But he turned when safe on the other side
> And built a bridge to span the tide.

> "Old man," said a fellow pilgrim near,
> "You are wasting your strength with building here;
> Your journey will end with the evening day,
> You never again will pass this way;
> You've crossed the chasm, deep and wide,
> Why build this bridge at evening tide?"

> The builder lifted his old gray head;
> "Good friend, in the path I have come," he said,
> "There followed after me to-day
> A youth whose feet must pass this way.
> This chasm that has been naught to me
> To that fair-haired youth may a pitfall be;
> He, too, must cross in the twilight dim;
> Good friend, I am building the bridge for him!"

As most of you know, Heady became incapacitated soon after
the second ISU-Thai project was officially in place, making this poem
even more meaningful to those of us directly involved in the projects.

He built the bridge. The impact that his students and their associates have had, are having, and will continue to have on agriculture and agricultural development in Thailand will be a far more meaningful tribute to Dr. Earl O. Heady than any words I can put together to describe his impact on a nation.

REFERENCE

Nicol, Kenneth J., Somnuk Sriplung, and Earl O. Heady, eds. 1982. *Agricultural Development Planning in Thailand.* Ames: Iowa State University Press.

GLENN L. JOHNSON

13

Two Reviews of
Economics of Agricultural Production
and Resource Use

M any references have been made throughout the previous
chapters to Earl O. Heady's book, *Economics of Agricultural
Production and Resource Use,* published in 1952 by Prentice
Hall. The following reviews by Glenn L. Johnson were originally
published in the *Australian Journal of Agricultural Economics* in 1963 and
in the *Journal of Agricultural Economics* in 1987. Hence, they should be
interpreted in their respective time frames. Earl Heady was always
critical of his own work and welcomed the constructive criticism of his
colleagues. These reviews help place the significance of "The Blue
Book" in the context of the field of production economics and in
relation to the contributions of others.

Glenn L. Johnson is Professor Emeritus, Michigan State University.

This review is reprinted from the *Australian Journal of Agricultural Economics,*
7(June 1963):12–26.

Stress on Production Economics

T his article was written at the invitation of the Editor of this
Journal. In earlier correspondence the point was made that the
author had been "having second thoughts on the decline of
some departments of agricultural economics which were of a more
applied nature" and that "this year will mark a decade since the
emergence of Earl Heady's massive tome," *Economics of Agricultural
Production and Resource Use,* Prentice Hall, Inc., New Jersey, 1952. The
suggestion was made to the author "that perhaps you could review
developments in the field of production economics since the birth of
the Heady *opus.*"

Preferably, the article should be viewed as critical of certain
developments in our profession, the origins of which extend back in
history prior to the lives of any living person and horizontally in our
society beyond the realms of production economics and, for that
matter, far beyond the social science disciplines. The need is for criticism of a development and not for criticism of the people who participated in the development.

HISTORICAL BACKGROUND

In reviews of this type, it is extremely important to establish and
interpret the historical context in which the developments under review take place. Therefore, the initial pages of this paper are devoted
to establishing and interpreting the historical setting in which Heady's
book was produced and used.

Historically, the discipline of agricultural economics grew out of
an interest in farm management on the part of agricultural technical
scientists. Those scientists became interested in the overall operation
of farm businesses and proceeded to develop a discipline of farm
management without relating the new discipline directly to econom-

ics.[1] Later, a number of agriculturalists trained in economics became interested in transferring theoretical economics into the emerging field of study, farm management. Important among these early U.S. contributors to the emerging discipline was Henry Taylor.[2,3] Somewhat later, John D. Black took up the case for economics in the field of farm management. Black's early contributions were made at Minnesota. Later, as a professor at Harvard, he stressed the need for more economics both in farm management and in the emerging departments of agricultural economics which were beginning to address themselves to problems in marketing, agricultural policy and agricultural prices.[4]

As a Harvard professor, Black was able to make the case for more economics in agricultural economics. Workers in marketing, agricultural policy and price analysis quickly became allies of anyone propounding the use of more economics in a college of agriculture. However, workers in the field of farm management proper resisted. They had strong constituent support among the farmers they serviced well and academic support in the allied technical agricultural disciplines from whence they came. Though these workers employed very little economic theory, they contributed to the solution of many problems facing farmers with relevant information from their accounting and descriptive work and a substantial quantity of common sense. No one can deny that the earlier, non-theoretical farm management workers made real contributions to agriculture, contributions which developed much financial support for the emerging discipline of agricultural economics, a debt not yet adequately recognized.

As just noted, the early descriptive, non-theoretical work in farm management was relevant for the solution of practical problems. The philosophy of science which guided these people was expressed in Karl Pearson's *Grammar of Science* and, as such, was essentially positivistic.[5] Though positivism avoids purpose and leads eventually to difficulty in defining and solving problems,[6] the charge of irrelevance could not be levelled validly at the early farm management workers. The closeness of these workers to farmers and their problems insured that the positivistic work they did involved the determination of facts which were relevant to the solution of problems facing farmers. However, with the passage of time, the interests of these workers and their successors became introverted instead of focused on problems.[7] Much of the descriptive work began to be done for its own sake, *i.e.*, it concentrated upon repetitive surveys and reports. Essentially, the same pattern of facts was gathered from account keepers and coopera-tors in surveys, while times and problems changed violently in the 1920's and 1930's.[8] This loss of relevance disturbed those desiring to make a greater place for economic theory in farm management work.

In 1939, T. W. Schultz added to the criticism.[9] He noted that farm management work failed to use economics to focus on the prob-lems of the post–World War I and depression years. He also noted that static economic theory, even where used, was not always appro-priate and called attention to the theory of the managerial processes expounded by Frank Knight in his *Risk, Uncertainty and Profit.* Though the main impact of Schultz's work was to strengthen the case for theory in farm management, his observations about the inappropri-ateness of static production economic theory in solving certain prob-lems were astute; they anticipate criticisms of production economics research to be advanced in later pages of this article. More specifically, these later pages will be concerned with lack of attention to problems not definable in terms of static disequilibria. Schultz also stressed that the work of departments and sections of farm management was vul-nerable on another score. Attention had been concentrated on the individual farm firm at the expense of dynamic and more macro or aggregative studies of the agricultural economy.[10] Still further, serious questions existed about sampling technique.[11] Statistically trained ag-ricultural economists, therefore, joined the chorus by criticizing the statistical methodologies and technique employed in both farm man-agement survey and farm records work.

After World War II, the irrelevance of much of the positivistic farm management accounting and survey work was clearly apparent to agricultural economists and to administrators.[12] The older or "tra-ditional" type of farm management fell in administrative esteem. Those pre-war departments of farm management, which had existed independently of departments of agricultural economics, were merged with those departments and, for the most part, lost their identity under administrators more fully committed to the use of economics in farm management.[13]

This submersion of farm management into agricultural econom-ics continued to occur intellectually as well as administratively. In the

North Central states, the Farm Foundation took steps in 1948 to organize a workshop at Land O'Lakes, Wisconsin. At that workshop, the earlier forms of farm management work were subjected to serious intellectual examination. The examination started at Land O'Lakes was continued at the Blackduck workshop a year later in Minnesota.

Though the issue at Land O'Lakes and Blackduck has often been interpreted as one between theorists and practitioners,[14] no person, to the writer's knowledge, has interpreted it as a difference between a positivistic philosophy, which tends eventually to preclude problem definition and problem solving as integral parts of the scientific method, and a more normative philosophy leading to work with value concepts, at least to the extent of assuming the existence of values in terms of which problems could be defined and solved.[15] However, it is easy to find quotations in the report of the Blackduck workshop which indicate that there was a concern at that conference with failures to define and solve problems.[16] These quotations contain clear evidence of a desire on the part of the theorists to focus farm management research in a "pinpoint manner" on problematic questions rather than employing "buckshot" farm accounts and surveys which produce, repetitively, a stable pattern of data not focused on the solution of any particular problem. At the Blackduck conference, efforts were made to isolate problems which could be solved by finding the equilibria defined in static production economic theory. Such use of economic theory assumed purpose and, as compared with positivistic survey and accounting work, *increased ability both to define and recognize solutions to problems involving attainment of the assumed purposes.* This, not theory *per se,* was what was attractive to those advocating the use of more theory. Such use of theory contrasted sharply with the endless, less *purposeful,* unchanging repetitive accumulation of farm survey and record data unfocused on the changing problems of farmers and society.

Though the new orientation concentrated on problems and, in this sense, differed significantly from the immediately preceding fact-finding research in the field of farm management, it contained a serious flaw to be discussed later. The flaw involved the narrowness of the problems considered which tended to be defined in terms of the disequilibria of static, production economic theory. This concentration made farm management a narrow problem-solving subfield of production economics which, in turn, was a subfield of general economics. Thus, even the initial problematic interests of the new theoretical farm management workers were narrower than those of the early, more traditional farm management workers whose interests had ranged from the technological and institutional through accounting to the sociological.[17]

The issue was carried back to the individual experiment stations and departments. In the years which followed, the older farm management members of the North Central Farm Management Research Committee retired and were replaced by persons with greater interest in economic theory and in statistics. Eventually, the North Central Farm Management Research Committee and much of the farm management research and teaching in Midwestern agricultural experiment stations developed an initial problem-solving orientation built around a substantial injection of economic theory into the field of farm management.

HEADY'S BOOK APPEARS

The historical perspective provided above indicates that agricultural economics (including the somewhat attenuated farm management groups) was well prepared for and, in fact, demanding the kind of book which Heady produced. Heady sensed and filled that demand. The alacrity with which this reviewer and many others adopted it as a graduate text attests to the esteem in which it was and is still held. This alacrity also reflected the widespread consensus in the profession about the need for the book. In reviewing the book, David MacFarlane wrote, "Professor Heady has written a highly important book . . . which for the first time brings within the covers of one volume the 'revolution' that has occurred in the field of agricultural production economics over the past 15 years. A small group of able, venturesome workers in farm management and production economics, with the author (Heady) in the forefront, have brought the 'new economics' to bear on farm production problems in an original and most valuable manner."[18]

The book articulated, in a remarkably accurate way, the then prevalent mood of the members of the profession, most of whom

viewed it as a means of bringing into use the powerful tools of economic theory in *defining* and *solving* the practical, important production *problems* of the agricultural economy, particularly at the individual
farm level. This was the driving purpose, the *raison d'etre*, of those who
eagerly adopted the text and built courses around it and the related
literature.

Ten years have now passed, and it is time to ask and answer the
question "Is production economics playing its proper role in agricultural economics, including farm management?"

To answer this question requires that we also outline the main
developments which have taken place since the appearance of the
book, that date having significance *not* because a book was published
at that time *but, instead, because* it more or less marks the triumph of a
point of view started by Spillman and Taylor, nurtured by Black, and
brought to triumph by Heady and others.

TRENDS SINCE THE TRIUMPH—A LOSS IN PRODUCTIVITY

Since 1952, the following trends have become evident in the
United States:

1. The use of economic theory in farm management *research* has
expanded many fold.

2. The use of advanced statistics, mathematics, and electronic
computers in farm management *research* has expanded far beyond
levels envisioned in the early 'fifties.

3. Farm management research with a "production-economics"
orientation has become increasingly:

    (a) less focused on the practical problem of managing
farms, and

    (b) more focused on methodological and theoretical issues
of less and less relevance to the solution of practical farm management problems as exemplified by such studies as joint input-
output experiments in crop and livestock production;[19] studies of
the managerial process, *per se;*[20] and budgeting and linear programming studies of farm organization.

4. The proportionate use of farm management research by ex-

tension workers has decreased as its production economics orientation has increased. This is associated with:

(a) decreased relevance in practical farm management problem situations of much of the current production economics research in farm management; and

(b) the failure to increase competence with respect to production economics as rapidly among extension as among research farm management workers.

5. Accompanying the above trends in farm management research toward methodological and theoretical research, at the expense of the practical, has been an expanded interest in macro and policy work on the part of the persons with specific training in production economics. There has also been an important but not comparable reciprocal interest of students of policy, prices, etc. in production economics. This macro and policy work has tended, in turn, to focus on the theoretical and methodological at the expense of the practical and applied,[21] and as such differs from a "natural" tendency of young farm management workers and others to develop an interest in policy.

6. "Production economics"–oriented farm management workers have either largely ignored or been largely ignored by the editors of the Journal of Farm Managers and Rural Appraisers, whose supporting association and membership have maintained a keen interest in the practical problems of farmers.

Somehow or another, these trends are not in accord with the expectations accompanying the shift to problem-solving farm management research based on the use of more theory. There has been no major rush of farmers to obtain the results of agronomic-economic research or of similar research in animal husbandry.[22] Production function and linear programming analyses of farm businesses have produced no major breakthrough.[23] T. W. Schultz has stated:

> It will be said that much progress has been made in production economics. Simple, old-fashioned budgeting has been replaced by sophisticated production functions. The journals runneth over with "results" from linear programming, a new apparatus that is turning out thus far an undigested mixture of a few insights and many "numbers" that do not make sense.[24]

The shifts to estimating supply responses from linear programmes and to stress on Leontief input-output studies have had little
impact on policy-makers.[25] In short, neither public nor private decision-makers have had much direct help from production economists
in solving problems. Lest this conclusion dismay production economists and farm management workers to the comfort of others, it is
worthwhile noting that, in 1959, a Committee of the Social Science
Research Council (S.S.R.C.) drew a similar conclusion about the
profession as a whole when it stated:

> Agriculture in the United States is in a period of critical change.
> The forces of change include rapid technological advance, rapid growth
> and structural change in the industrial and commercial environment
> within which agriculture functions, and an accompanying intensifica-
> tion and realignment of political pressure impinging on agricultural
> policy.
>
> . . . The economic and social consequences of these changes in
> agriculture are far-reaching and arouse widespread concern. These con-
> sequences include serious chronic distress within major sectors of agri-
> culture itself, in spite of public remedial programmes that have grown to
> unmanageable proportions, and an accelerated movement of popula-
> tion out of agriculture that nevertheless appears to fall short of the rate
> needed for economic adjustment. Among families that remain in agri-
> culture, the income gap widens between those able to adopt progressive
> technology and those lacking the necessary financial resources or per-
> sonal capabilities. Successive sectors of agriculture are being increas-
> ingly controlled by outside commercial interests. Areas of traditional
> economic leadership in agriculture are challenged by new areas of agri-
> cultural economic growth.
>
> The concern with these consequences reaches all strata of the
> agricultural population and all groups concerned with agricultural wel-
> fare. . . .
>
> There are, of course, no simple, easily applied, costless, yet effec-
> tive remedies for agriculture's ills. But they are not beyond constructive
> approach. That comments are so often only doctrinaire and that argu-
> ments seem so repetitious suggest *failure on the part of agricultural economists
> to apply imagination, to depart from customary thought patterns, to break down the
> mental barriers that restrict their formulation of problems.*[26] (Italics mine.)

If we accept the truth of the S.S.R.C. committee statement and
the earlier criticisms which were directed more specifically at production economists and their work, then all agricultural economists as

well as production economists must ask, Why? Why has the increased theoretical and empirical competence of agricultural economists led to reduced instead of increased productivity in terms of ability "to apply imagination, to depart from customary thought patterns, and to break down the mental barriers that restrict their formulation of problems"?[27] Or more specifically, on the subject of this paper, why have the production economists' efforts to include more production economics theory and improved mathematical and/or statistical methods in farm management and in other phases of agricultural economics been accompanied by less rather than more productivity?

WHY

Two explanations for the irrelevance (and, hence, reduced ability to contribute to solutions of practical problems) of much current production economics research work in farm management and other phases of agricultural economics are to be found not in production economics itself, but instead in specialization in economics and a tendency to become more positivistic.[28]

These two developments, as we saw earlier, are in part consequences of an environmental call for more emphasis on production economics and, as such, can hardly be regarded as consequences of that emphasis or as a sole responsibility of those who answered the call. It is likely that these developments explain the lack of productivity in general agricultural economics which concerned Brinegar and his co-authors in the S.S.R.C. committee report.

Specialization in economics has a tendency to result in concentration on problems of economic disequilibria to the exclusion of other kinds of problems.[29] In economic theory, disequilibria indicate that problems exist. Problems definable in terms of disequilibria are solvable with recommendations designed to establish equilibria. So long as the marginality conditions for an equilibrium are met, the problems which exist are not directly discernible or solvable solely within the theory and, hence, tend to be overlooked by persons concentrating on the use of such theory.

The theory, for instance, does not ask whether the equilibrium distribution of incomes resulting from a given initial asset ownership pattern constitutes a problem or not. Though the core of a Kentucky hill farmer's problem be that of getting ownership of enough property and command over enough skill to earn "a decent living," no purely "economic problem" exists if his hill farm is organized to "equate returns at the margin in both his production and consumption activities." While there is an income problem solvable by helping the Kentucky hill farmer get control "by hook or by crook" over more property and skills, the focus of economic theory on disequilibria tends to distract its user's attention away from the really relevant problem of inadequate resources in a search for non-existent problems of disequilibria.

When the problem is one of changing the institutional structure of agriculture, problems of disequilibria, too, are likely to be present but often are not worth correcting until the institutional changes are made, at which time new disequilibria are likely to arise to render irrelevant the original problems of disequilibria. For instance, in recent decades the problems encountered in designing new farm credit institutions and in creating institutional arrangements for controlling soil erosion were not solely problems of disequilibria and were more likely to create new equilibria than to cure old ones.

Similarly, a problem growing out of a need to discover or create new technology may exist whether or not a farm business is in equilibrium. And, the discovery or creation would, in turn, typically obviate any pre-existing equilibria or disequilibria, possibly leaving a still greater disequilibrium problem to be solved as a minor subconsequence of the solution to the major farm management problem. The tendency to reduce farm management to a subfield of production economics, which is, in turn, a subfield of economics shows up in the work of J. D. Black who wrote in 1953, "When the economics of agricultural production is reduced to terms of the individual farm, it becomes what is ordinarily known as Farm Management. Any textbook in *real* (my italics) Farm Management is a treatise on the economics of production of the individual farm."[30]

These examples should be sufficient to make it clear that concentration on problems of economic disequilibria is not identical with concentration on important, relevant problems. In fact, it is argued here that the problems which dismayed the S.S.R.C. sub-committee were mainly of this variety and that they were being ignored by agricultural economists who had concentrated instead on problems of disequilibria.

In 1959, this author commented,

> The tendency of farm management workers to oversimplify by concentrating on static economic analysis . . . is of recent origin. Somehow or another we have become so concerned with technique and simplicity that we fail to face up to problems either practically or methodologically. . . . We do repetitive applications of mechanistic techniques sometimes using hypothetical data. In short, we play with technique and underemphasize the descriptive as a basis for isolating problems and preparing an all out attack on them . . . we fail to face up to the non-Pareto-better aspects of technological advance, economic growth and uncertainty . . . and of changes in wants and preferences.[31]

We now turn to the tendency toward positivism as a second explanation of the irrelevance of much research work involving production economics. This tendency is, of course, the same one which led earlier, nontheoretical farm management away from the relevant to the irrelevant.

The *tendency toward positivism* has gone through several stages in economic investigations involving the use of theory.

Early, Pareto and Hicks recognized the problem of assessing gains conferred on some persons in terms comparable with assessments of losses imposed on others. Without such assessments, it is difficult to ascertain whether a proposed solution to a problem would result in a net gain or loss. Recognition of this measurement problem suggested the advisability of limiting conclusions about net gains to situations in which at least one person was made better off and *no one* was made worse off. Use of "the compensation principle" made it possible to extend the conclusion to instances where compensation could be paid by those benefited to anyone damaged and still leave those benefited better off. This development reduced the number of decisions which economists were willing to make about which actions are "right" to take or recommend as solutions to practical problems. Solutions were precluded which involved the imposition of uncompensatable damages on one or more persons or groups in order to benefit others.[32] The preclusion of such solutions leads to avoidance of problems involving institutional changes, redistribution of property rights and income streams, technological advance, and education advances.

Pareto's and Hicks' recognition of the problem of obtaining interpersonally valid utility measurements prepared the ground for the acceptance of the still more drastic positivistic conclusion that nothing objective was knowable about purpose, about good and bad, or, for that matter, about right and wrong solutions to problems. The research methodologies implied by positivism were and are extremely productive in the physical sciences where normative questions are less obvious and immediate than in the applied and/or social science disciplines. In fact, animistic and teleological reasoning which are non-positivistic but, fortunately, not the only kinds of non-positivistic reasoning often hinder non-social science research by introducing purely imaginary "purpose" to distract and, hence, lower the productivity of investigators. From this point, it is easy, if erroneous, to conclude that positivistic methodologies should be embraced to the exclusion of the normative in order to gain for social science the productivity of the physical sciences.

It was a long way *from the pre-Pareto and pre-Hicksian point of view* that objective knowledge of good and bad exists and is attainable *to the positivistic point of view* that such knowledge does not exist and, hence, is unattainable. It is a road from having some confidence in an objective ability to define and prescribe the solution to problems, to making both the definition and the solution of problems matters of subjective opinion beyond the realm of objective inquiry. So viewed problem-solving research loses its dignity, and is referred to as applied (the slang term is "putting out brush fires"), while positivistic research is glorified as "basic and fundamental." Paradoxically, the probability of relevance for what is called basic and fundamental yet divorced from the problems of society, seems to approach zero as only a small part of the infinitely complex, real and imaginal world is relevant.

One of the intermediate stages on the road from problem-solving to extreme positivism involves the technique of assuming or taking as given what is good and bad and then defining problems as involving the maximization of the good or minimization of the bad. This technique, referred to elsewhere by this author as "conditional normativism,"[33] was more widely used by production economists formerly than now but is still followed extensively.

Kenneth Parsons has attacked conditionally normative research in a recent article.[34] Parsons feels that if researchers do not proceed under the proposition that knowledge of right and wrong is possible, they will become unproductive. Parsons' own specialized pragmatic philosophy holds that answers to normative and non-normative questions are inextricably interdependent and that to assume one while varying the other is impossible. In contrast to Parsons, Ciriacy-Wantrup urged production economists to become more positivistic.[35]

With or without Ciriacy-Wantrup's urging, the tendency has been for some production economists to be more positivistic. Distinctions are now being drawn between *supply functions,* which are defined as what profit maximizing farmers ought to do, and *supply response estimates,* which predict what farmers will actually do. The first are labelled normative, while the latter are dubbed positive or predictive. In commenting on an assignment to discuss normative supply functions, this author once wrote:

> The term "Normative," which appears in the title, has unfortu-
> nately tended to become an opprobrious epithet reserved in certain
> circles for *inaccurate* supply estimates while accurate estimates are labelled
> "predictive" or "positive." This unfortunate distinction arises from the
> desire of positivists to avoid purpose or ends as being animistic, teleolog-
> ical and, hence, non-scientific (in their opinion). The use of this distinc-
> tion implies that the behaviour of producers can be accurately predicted
> without reference to desire for profit, liquidity preference, desires for
> security as reflected in risk discounts, and the desires for security as
> reflected in willingness to make long chance investments which condi-
> tion the behaviour of producers. The author feels that appropriate han-
> dling of subjective matters involving purposes and ends will produce
> more accurate (in the positivistic sense) supply response estimates than
> attempts to eliminate consideration of such matters. Obviously, studies
> which assume entrepreneurs to maximize what they do not, in fact, try
> to maximize may produce at least as inaccurate estimates as studies
> which avoid all maximization. Human behaviour (and production deci-
> sions are a form of human behaviour) is often a compromise between
> the entrepreneurs, concepts about "what ought to be" (values or norms)
> and concepts about "what is or can be" (beliefs — facts or predicted facts).
> It seems obvious that more accurate predictions of facts about supply
> decisions and responses must, generally speaking, be obtained in studies
> which take both values and beliefs into account than by non-normative
> studies. In addition, of course, errors in the process by which "right
> actions" are determined from value and belief concepts would have to be

considered in order to arrive at still more accurate predictions. The point is that the behaviour of producers is in part a social phenomenon, "a serious analysis" of which, in Knight's words, requires "a quite complicated pluralism," including but not limited to positivism. . . .[36]

On the relative objectivity of normative and non-normative concept formulation Boulding has written "Although I shall argue that the process by which we obtain an image of values is not very different from the process whereby we obtain an image of fact, there is clearly a certain difference between them.[37]

A conference of the Iowa Adjustment Center, recognized the inadequacy of positive research by focusing on goals and values. As Director of the Center for Agricultural and Economic Adjustment, Heady wrote, "Until it is recognized that progress to solution of the income problem rests on resolution of apparent conflicts in goals and values, progress in solving major structural problems of agriculture may be small."[38] The importance of normative considerations in defining and solving problems which Heady recognized in the above quotation has been underscored in a large number of recent reports,[39] even if not reflected in the nature and content of much current production economics research which has, instead, tended toward the positivistic at the expense of the conditionally normative and normative. This tendency toward positivism has led us away from relevant problem-solving work.

In summary, then, this long section supports the thesis that specialization and a tendency towards positivism are responsible for the lack of productivity (in terms of solving problems) noted in the previous section.

As constructive criticism demands corrective suggestions, the next step is to examine some of the problems being neglected as a prelude to suggesting some needed redirection in the last section.

EXAMPLES OF THE KINDS OF PROBLEMS
WHICH ARE NOT BEING HANDLED

As problem situations are dynamic and not static, a stable list of neglected problems cannot be produced. Thus, the following partial list of specific problems is necessarily ephemeral and only illustrative.

In the *problem area of farm management,* production economists can contribute to the solution of problems:

1. faced by technical researchers asking what kind of new technologies are needed;

2. faced by farmers unsure about the value to be placed on security, income, the "fringe benefits" of urban society, education, public facilities, research, etc.[40]

3. faced by farmers in different regions when changes are proposed which would influence their comparative advantages. Such changes include modifications of transportation, technology, production control and price support schemes, credit institutions, international trade arrangements, *etc.;*

4. faced by farmers without command over enough resources to enable them to earn acceptable incomes in equilibrium. Here the need may be for access (right) to more credit, outright ownership of more property, command (ownership) of more skills, use (right to, ownership of) more public or semi-public property such as roads, schools, market facilities, research agencies, and accounting systems. The production economist can help predict the consequences of such changes and contribute substantially to conclusions about their desirability even when the changes under consideration are obviously non-Pareto-better;

5. faced by farmers locally, seasonally and chronically short of labour or priced out of the labour market. In this connection, work is needed (a) on institutional arrangements affecting the seasonal and geographical supply of labour, (b) on farm reorganization plans affecting labour utilization (such plans involving far more than shifts on given subproduction functions), and (c) by technical researchers on what kinds of labour saving technology are needed.

Without exploring all the ramifications of these and other farm management problems, some attention should be given to the kinds of marketing problems which production economists can help solve. Roughly, these parallel those in farm management and, like those in that area, are often not definable in terms of initial disequilibria. In fact, marketing situations in initial equilibrium may often call for drastic changes.

1. In both factor and product markets, situations reach static impasses where drastic action is required. Present product markets are not characterized by widespread disequilibria, given existing government controls, yet there is an active search for new market arrangements and mechanisms. In Michigan, for instance the Farm Bureau actively seeks, through its farm service organization, new bargaining rights for farmers producing processing apples, pickles and sugar beets. Elsewhere in the U.S., bargaining rights are sought by a new major farm organization, the National Farmers Organization, for livestock products and for food grains. What are production economists doing with respect to problems involving new ways of producing marketing services, reorganizing markets and devising new marketing mechanisms?

2. The labour market, too, is characterized by demands for new arrangements for handling foreign and domestic migrant labourers to meet seasonal, local and regional shortages of labour. Production economists have much to offer in predicting the consequences of alternative solutions and in estimating the disequilibria which would be created by various proposed changes.

3. In marketing, too, there is great interest in new physical layouts and technologies to reduce labour requirements. What production economists have really become creative and aggressive in developing such layouts and in indicating to engineers and architects the kind of equipment and buildings required?

Economic development and growth has always been a major concern of agricultural economists. Farm economies, stagnating in near static equilibria, are characteristic of many of the underdeveloped countries. People can be starving and going without the elemental requirements for supra-animal existence in "penny capitalistic" economies which are in equilibria.[41] The problems here involve changes in land tenure, additional ownership of capital, new skills, and rights to new services. Introduction to these changes, in turn destroys old equilibria whose existence paralyzes the thoughts of economists trying to find infinitesimal problems of disequilibria while walking over mountains of problems involving human suffering, injustice and hopeless despair. Especially in economic development, normative work is badly needed to clarify and establish (by experience and logic) the workability of various concepts of the goodness and badness of such things as income, medical facilities, lawfulness, disorderliness, justice, work, education, *etc.*

Agricultural policy also presents a wide range of problems, only part of which involve disequilibria and most of which involve serious normative questions. Here we have problems involving public investment in agricultural research; the creation of institutions to stabilize production and prices, public investment in roads, irrigation and drainage facilities, and education; the procurement and/or maintenance of rights to services such as electricity, telephones, markets, schools, *etc.*, as size of farms increases and population densities decrease. We also have problems of devising new institutional ways of controlling resource flows into and out of agriculture. The production economist has much help to offer in estimating and evaluating the output effects of such alternative policies and programmes if he will face up to such problems.

NEEDED REDIRECTIONS

All of the above has noted two current tendencies:

1. of production economics researchers (and others acquiring increased theoretical and empirical competence) to specialize in problems of disequilibria to the *exclusion* of problems involving technical, political, social and other changes; and

2. of production economics researchers to become increasingly positivistic to the *exclusion* of normative investigations.

Fortunately, neither tendency has become completely dominant though both have reduced the relevance of the research work of production economists and others stressing theoretical and empirical competence. The needed redirections do not involve either a change in or a diminished total role for production economics. Instead, they involve:

1. the use of production economics in conjunction with data and concepts from a wide range of academic disciplines to attack a wide

range of practical problems going far beyond conventional economic disequilibria;

2. the avoidance of the sterilizing impacts of highly specialized philosophies of inquiry, particularly positivism, with its presumption that objective knowledge of purpose, of good and bad, or right and wrong is unobtainable;

3. recognition that the wide range of problems to be attacked by production economists which is beyond economic disequilibria requires related research in the physical and social sciences and in the humanities; thus, the contribution of production economists to problem-solving research needs to be recognized as *partial* within problematic areas much broader than production economics or, for that matter, all of economics.

So directed, the contribution of production economics can fulfill the hopes of that "small group of able and venturesome workers in farm management and production economics, with the author (Heady) of this volume in the forefront" who "brought the new economics to bear on farm production problems in an original and most valuable manner."[42] At the time Heady's book was written, the reviewer just quoted also wrote, "Our definition and understanding of problems is more revealing; and our tools sharper. For these advances we owe a tremendous debt to Professor Heady." Now, over ten years later, I would write instead, "Professor Heady's book has increased our capacity to understand and find problems and has sharpened our tools. For this we owe Professor Heady a tremendous debt. Whether or not we use this capacity to understand and find and help *solve* the important problems of private and public decision makers depends upon *our* ability to use these tools without being confined to them and without becoming unduly positivistic as our account keeping and/or surveying forebears did before us. This performance we came dangerously close to repeating during the last half of the decade which has passed since Professor Heady made his truly great contribution to agriculture."

NOTES

The paper has benefited from criticisms and suggestions received from Lowell Hardin, Sam Engene, Dale Hathaway, Vernon Sorenson, L. L. Boger, James Bonnen, Carl Eicher, Karl Wright, Robert Jones and others. The content, however, remains the sole responsibility of the author.

1. Walter Wilcox, Sherman Johnson and Stanley Warren, *Farm Management Research 1940–41*, Social Science Research Council, New York, N.Y., Bull. 52, 1943, pp. 1–4.

2. J. R. Currie, "A Review of Fifty Years in Farm Management Research," *Journal of Agricultural Economics*, Vol. XI, 1955 ". . . the first serious scientific studies of the economics of farming . . . started in the United States of America."

3. Wilcox, Johnson and Warren, *op. cit.* p. 4.

4. J. D. Black, *Introduction to Production Economics*, Henry Holt and Co., New York, 1926; and J. D. Black and A. G. Black, *Production Organization*, Henry Holt and Co., New York, 1929.

5. By positivistic, the author means, "the philosophic position that the highest form of knowledge is simple description." *The Dictionary of Philosophy — Ancient — Medieval — Modern*, edited by D. D. Reeves. Littlefield, Adams & Co., Patterson, N.J., U.S.A., 1961, p. 243. This position ordinarily holds that goodness and badness are not observable and, hence, not susceptible to description.

6. Purpose is rejected as teleological and nonexplanatory.

7. A similar situation developed in land economics when a pragmatic "problem-solving" approach competed with a positivistic approach. See L. A. Salter, *A Critical Review of Research in Land Economics*, The University of Minnesota Press, Minneapolis, 1948, pp. 39ff.

8. Wilcox, *et al., op. cit.* preface by T. W. Schultz, p. viii.

9. T. W. Schultz, "Scope and Method in Agricultural Economics Research," *Journal of Political Economy*. Vol. XLVII, 1939, pp. 709ff.

10. Wilcox, *et al., op. cit.* preface.

11. *Ibid*, p. vii and last full paragraph continuing on p. viii.

12. Farm accounting and surveys not focused directly on problems (either practical or academic) fell off. In Michigan, for instance, the number of farm accounts was reduced from 862 in 1948 to 501 in 1953.

13. Glenn L. Johnson, "Agricultural Economics, Production Economics and the Field of Farm Management," *Journal of Farm Economics*, Vol. 39, May 1957, pp. 441ff. Also, H. C. M. Case and D. B. Williams, *Fifty Years of Farm Management*, University of Illinois Press, Urbana, Illinois, 1957, pp. 319ff.

14. Case and Williams, *op. cit.* pp. 359–63 and 366ff.

15. Case and Williams, *ibid.,* come close to recognizing that the traditional approach was positivistic but do not really clarify the matter. See p. 360 for a discussion of "The emphasis on fact collection . . . inherited from the physical sciences."

16. Report of the North Central Farm Management Research Workshop, August 22 to September 2, 1949. The focus on problems is clearly discernible in the discussion of the theory of research which produced an outline containing the following:

Selecting the Study. The study should be selected with a view toward: (a) solving specific, definable problems leading to purposeful action; (b) anticipating problems and discovering remedies before they arise . . .

The problem selected for study should be significant in terms of; (a) its own importance and/or acuteness and (b) its relationship to other problems . . .

Stating the Problem. The problem should be stated clearly and fully in terms of: (a) the nature and extent of the apparent situation; (b) the circumstances which give rise to it; (c) the limitations and presuppositions under which it will be pursued; (d) the application expected to be made of the results; and (e) the economic ends of the individual or society . . .

Determining the Evidence Needed. The evidence to be assembled should: (a) be relevant to the stated problem and hypotheses . . .

Presenting the Results . . . Forthright endeavours should be made to insure utilization of the findings: (a) by obtaining and maintaining contacts with press, radio, extension workers, and other outlets; (b) by presenting the findings to persons in strategic positions; (c) by sharing experiences with fellow workers through personal contacts, journal articles, correspondence, *etc.*

17. As evidenced by the number of rural sociology departments which grew out of the activities of administrators of the earlier, more traditional farm management departments, those departments having evolved earlier out of the technological departments.

18. See David D. MacFarlane's highly complimentary review in the *Journal of Farm Economics,* August 1953, Vol. 35, p. 445.

19. Compare E. L. Baum, *et al.* (eds.), *Methodological Procedures in the Economic Analysis of Fertilizer Use Data,* Iowa State University Press. Ames, Iowa, 1955, with E. L. Baum, *et al.* (eds.), *Economic and Technical Analysis of Fertilizer Innovations and Resource Use,* Iowa State University Press, Ames, Iowa 1957.

20. Compare G. L. Johnson and C. B. Haver, *Decision-Making Principles in Farm Management,* Kentucky Agricultural Experiment Station Bulletin, January 1953, with G. L. Johnson *et al.,* (eds.), *A Study of Managerial Processes of Midwestern Farmers,* Iowa State University Press, Ames, Iowa, 1961.

21. Compare E. O. Heady, *et al.* (eds.) *Agricultural Adjustment Problems in a Growing Economy,* Iowa State University Press, Ames, Iowa 1958, with E. O. Heady, *et al.* (eds.) *Agricultural Supply Functions—Estimating Techniques and Interpretations,* Iowa State University Press, Ames, Iowa, 1961.

22. R. F. Hutton and D. W. Thorne, "Review Notes on the Heady-Pesek Fertilizer Production Surface," *Journal of Farm Economics,* Feb. 1955, Vol. 37, pp. 117ff. Also see G. L. Johnson, "A Critical Evaluation of Fertilizer Research," *The Economics of Fertilizer Application,* Farm Management Research Conference of the Western Agricultural Economics Research Council, Report No. 1, June 1956, pp. 33ff.

23. James S. Plaxico, "Problems of Factor-Product Aggregation in Cobb-Douglas Value Productivity Analysis," *Journal of Farm Economics,* November 1955, Vol.

37, pp. 664ff. Also see Earl Swanson, "Determining Optimum Size of Business from Production Functions," in E. O. Heady, *et al.* (eds.) *Resource Productivity, Returns to Scale and Farm Size,* Iowa State University Press, Ames, Iowa 1956, pp. 133ff.

24. T. W. Schultz, "Reflections on Agricultural Production, Output and Supply," in E. O. Heady, *et al.,* (eds.), *Economic and Technical Analysis of Fertilizer Innovations and Resource Use,* Iowa State University Press, Ames, Iowa 1957, p. 335. In this same connection see *Farm Size and Output Research — A Study in Research Methods,* Southern Coop. Series Bull. No. 56, June 1958, bottom of p. 118 and top of p. 119.

25. See T. W. Schultz, "Output-Input Relationships Revisited," *Journal of Farm Economics,* Nov. 1958, Vol. 40, pp. 924ff., which is critical of an earlier article of Heady's published in the May 1958 issue of the same journal. Heady had, in turn, criticized a still earlier article by Schultz in the August 1956 issue of the same journal.

26. George K. Brinegar, Kenneth L. Bachman and Herman M. Southworth, "Reorientations in Research in Agricultural Economics," *Journal of Farm Economics,* Vol. 41, August 1959, pp. 600ff. Other more polite but nonetheless disturbing papers include those of W. W. Cochrane, "Agricultural Economics in the Decade Ahead," — *Journal of Farm Economics,* Vol. 36, December 1954, pp. 817ff. and Karl Brandt, "The Orientation of Agricultural Economics," *Journal of Farm Economics,* December 1955, pp. 793ff.

27. *Ibid.* Brinegar, *et al. Journal of Farm Economics,* Aug. 1959, pp. 600ff.

28. *Ibid.* Brinegar, Bachman and Southworth, advance an alternative explanation, that of compartmentalization, which some readers may want to pursue. This explanation does not seem to be a very useful explanation of the lack of productivity associated with departmentalizing (the opposite of compartmentalization) farm management by making it more a part of economics. Disagreement with the SSRC Agricultural Economics committee point of view is also found in *Management Strategies in Great Plains Farming,* Great Plains Council Publication No. 19, published by the University of Nebraska College of Agriculture, August 1961, p. 97.

29. Glenn L. Johnson, Agricultural Economics, Production Economics and the Field of Farm Management, *Journal of Farm Economics,* Vol. 39, May 1957, pp. 441ff.

30. J. D. Black, *Introduction to Economics for Agriculture,* Macmillan Co., New York, 1953, p. 120; also see Johnson, *Ibid.*

31. *Management Strategies in Great Plains Farming, op. cit.* p. 98.

32. The work of the North Central Technical Committee (NC-28) on soil conservation concentrated on the Pareto-better aspects of conservation and missed the "real" problems which involve imposition of damages on the living to confer benefits on those yet unborn. See L. A. Bradford and Glenn L. Johnson, *Farm Management Analysis,* Wiley & Co., New York, 1953, p. 429, for a brief statement of this aspect of the soil conservation problem. Also see Glenn L. Johnson, *op. cit,* p. 14.

33. Glenn L. Johnson, "Value Problems in Farm Management," *Journal of Agricultural Economics,* Vol 14, June 1962, p. 13f. This article discusses conditional normativism in relation to modern welfare economics.

34. In this attack, he specifically and emphatically disagrees with the conditional normativism of J. D. Black and E. O. Heady. See, Kenneth Parsons, "The Value Problem in Agricultural Policy," in E. O. Heady, *et al.* (eds.) *Agricultural Adjustment Problems in a Growing Economy,* Iowa State University Press, Ames, Iowa 1958, pp. 195–196.

35. S. V. Ciriacy-Wantrup "Policy Considerations in Farm Management Research," *Journal of Farm Economics,* Vol. 38, pp. 1301ff.

36. Glenn L. Johnson, "Budgeting and Normative Analysis of Normative Supply Functions," in Earl O. Heady *et al.* (eds.) *Agricultural Supply Functions — Estimating Techniques and Interpretations,* Iowa State University Press, Ames, 1961, pp. 170–171. Frank Knight's interesting but somewhat contradictory position on this is found in his book *On the History and Method of Economics,* The University of Chicago Press, Chicago, 1956, Chapter VII, especially pp. 172–177.

37. Kenneth E. Boulding, *The Image,* The University of Michigan Press, Ann Arbor, Mich., 1956, p. 11.

38. Iowa State University Center for Agricultural and Economic Adjustment, *Goals and Values in Agricultural Policy,* Iowa State University Press, Ames, 1961, p. vi. At this conference, many conflicting positions on how to work with values and goals were presented and noted, emphatically, to be inconsistent. In this connection, see pp. 254ff.

These conflicts, in turn, were still apparent at a subsequent conference of the Center which was devoted to the *problem* of land use; one-half of one out of 22 chapters reporting that conference was devoted to normative considerations. See, Iowa State University Center for Agricultural and Economic Adjustment, *Dynamics of Land Use — Needed Adjustment,* Iowa State University Press, Ames, 1961. For a review of this effort, with emphasis on its normative shortcomings, see G. L. Johnson, "Dynamics of Land Use — Needed Adjustment — Review," *Journal of Farm Economics,* Vol. 44, May 1962, pp. 643ff.

39. Joseph Ackerman, *et al.* (eds.) *Land Economics Research,* Farm Foundation and Resources for the Future, Inc., Johns Hopkins Press, Baltimore, Maryland, 1962. See Chapters, 1, 3, 9 and 11. Also see *Land and Water Planning for Economic Growth,* Western Water Resources Conference, University of Colorado Press, 1961, pp. 129–136 and pp. 177ff. and Glenn L. Johnson and Lewis K. Zerby "Values in the Solution of Credit Problems," in E. L. Baum, *et al.* (eds.) *Capital and Credit Needs in a Changing Agriculture,* Iowa State University Press, Ames, 1961, pp. 271ff.

40. Dynamic production economists interested in the managerial process clearly have an interest in the "good judgment of managers." Judgment is asserted here to depend on knowledge of the value of income, security, *etc.*

41. Sol. Tax, *Penny Capitalism: A Guatemalan Indian Economy,* University of Chicago Press, Chicago, 1963.

42. MacFarlane, *op. cit.* p. 444.

Economics of Agricultural Production
and Resource Use
after 35 Years

BOOKS REVIEWED

Note from the Book Review Editor

I n our rush to keep up with new publications we sometimes forget their intellectual ancestry. We publish in this issue the first of a series of retrospective reviews of classic books in agricultural economics. They were selected by Fellows of the Association who were asked to identify the dozen or so books that have made the largest contribution to our profession. Over the next several years we will publish one or two of these retrospective reviews in most issues of the "Journal." The first review, by Glenn L. Johnson, is of the book that received the most nominations by the Fellows: Earl O. Heady's text on production economics.

A SECOND PERSPECTIVE ON EARL O. HEADY'S
*ECONOMICS OF AGRICULTURAL PRODUCTION
AND RESOURCE USE*
(Englewood Cliffs, NJ: Prentice Hall, 1952)

This is the second time I have been asked to provide a perspective review of Earl O. Heady's stellar *Economics of Agricultural Production and Resource Use.* My first review article was requested and published by the *Australian Journal of Agricultural Economics* in June 1963 and reprinted by the American Economics Association (Fox and Johnson). That review and an earlier very complimentary one by Mac-

This review is reprinted from the *American Journal of Agricultural Economics,*
69(August 1987):707–711.

Farlane provide a perspective it is unnecessary to repeat here. Consequently, I provide here only (a) information about the book's place in the history of agricultural and general economic thought not included in my 1963 article and (b) a perspective growing out of developments since 1963.[1]

Because I will deplore certain developments in agricultural production economics which started before 1963 and have continued since then, I want to start by stating I greatly admire both Heady and his book and do not hold them uniquely responsible for these developments. Heady's book improved and expanded the use of theory by agricultural economists, particularly in farm management—this was a great, much needed accomplishment. Just as important and meritorious, Heady and his book stressed empirical work. I doubt if any other book has succeeded in joining economic theory and empirical work so well in an area where such stress was so badly needed; in this sense, the book is a great econometrics book.

The long-term impact of Heady's book was partially determined by forces outside of it. It was a leading part—but only part—of the post–World War II agricultural production economics movement. That movement, in turn, was only part of agricultural economics, which was, in turn, only part of general economics. Both agricultural and general economics have been very volatile since 1952. And beyond economics was the rest of the social sciences, the so-called hard sciences, and society at large. At all of these levels, the 1952–87 period has been dynamic and characterized by sweeping vertically and horizontally interrelated change. Heady's book and post–World War II agricultural production economics movement as parts of this broad and deep pattern of development both influenced it and were influenced by it. The remarkable thing is the extent of the book's and Heady's strong positive influence in such a large dynamic domain.

I turn now to additional historical perspective on the book's relation to earlier and then current (1952) agricultural and general economic thought. Bernard F. Stanton correctly called attention to the relationship of Heady's book to Kenneth Boulding's *Economic Analysis* (1948). In addition to Boulding's influence, it should be noted that John R. Hicks' isoquant and related concepts were used extensively in the book. Hicks developed these to keep production and consumption economics parallel after weakening the latter by dropping the presumption of cardinal utility measures. The influence of Gerhard Tintner is also apparent in the book's empirical emphasis and its implied, if not explicit, orientation to axiomatization and the analytic/synthetic distinctions formulated by the logical positivists of Europe. However, to my knowledge there are no references to techniques for estimating the parameters of simultaneous equations or to reduced-form versus structural equations, although these techniques were developed before 1952. Carlson's *A Study on the Pure Theory of Production* is referenced, but Stigler's *Production and Distribution Theories* is not. There is a reference to Paul Samuelson's *Foundation of Economic Analysis,* a book some might regard as a beginning of what McCloskey (1983, 1985) now deplores as "modernism." There is also evidence of the impacts of Gunnar Myrdal's "conditional normativism" as expounded in his appendix 2, though Heady makes no specific reference to it. There are, however, references to Hicks' Parieto-optimality via the works of Arrow and Reder. Conditional normativism and Parieto-optimality are easily interpretable as variants of logical positivism (Johnson, 1986, p. 85). Talcott Parsons' influence (probably via the teaching of T. W. Schultz) is evident early in the book in the means/end diagram on page 4 and in the accompanying discussion. Mordecai Ezekiel's *Methods of Correlation Analysis* was probably influential, although specific references are absent. Wisconsonian institutionalism and its underlying pragmatism are neglected and exert little if any influence in the book. There are few if any references to institutionalism or to such institutionalists as John R. Commons, Richard T. Ely, Kenneth Parsons, Leon Salter, Ray Penn, and John Timmons or Ranier Schickele (both Iowa State University colleagues). With respect to the neglect of institutionalism, it should be remembered that at about this time Boulding is reported to have referred to institutional economics as a mixture of poor economics and bad sociology (or was it vice versa?) before delivering, considerably later, his presidential address to the American Economic Association (1969) in which he displayed a substantial amount of pragmatic institutionalism. Land and resource economics were a concern of Heady in his book but not in an institutionalist pragmatic manner.

In addition to its heavy orientation to post-Hicksian neoclassical (market-oriented) economic theory and empirical work, Heady's book can be characterized as: (a) having been written before many post–World War II techniques came into vogue, such as linear programming (there is only a rudimentary LP discussion based almost entirely on an inadequate comprehension of Koopman's book (*Activity Analysis of Production and Allocation*), input/output analysis, cost/benefit analysis, expected utility analysis, frontier production functions, and distributed lags; (b) having a logically positivistic orientation to the exclusion of the pragmatism of the institutional economists; (c) being dynamic mainly in the elementary sense of Frank Knight's and A. G. Hart's treatments of risk and uncertainty (the role and earnings of management are also treated in an elementary though infinitely better way than John D. Black did in his *Introduction to Production Economics* and than Black, Clawson, Sayre, and Wilcox did in their book *Farm Management*, both of which seriously neglected risk, uncertainty, and managerial theory); (d) having omitted the expected utility analysis of choices involving risk (Friedman and Savage, vonNeumann and Morgenstern); and (e) being primarily static in orientation to the neglect of such long-run forces for growth, stagnation, and deterioration of technical, institutional, and human change and even changes in the base of conventional man-made and natural resources.

Since my 1963 review of Heady's book, the agricultural production economics movement of which the book was an important part has continued both affecting and being affected by the academic and cultural environment of which it is a part. Even before 1963, there were indications that specialization of farm management on production economics was reducing the productivity of the former (Johnson, 1957). This has since become so apparent that a reincarnation of traditional (pre-production economics) farm management has re-evolved that is now referred to as "farming systems." This reincarnation originated with the biological and physical agricultural sciences that earlier begat farm management, which in turn had become too specialized and disciplinary to serve them (Ramaratnam, Johnson 1982).

This partial sterilization of farm management was not the only adverse impact of treating production economics and farm management as synonymous. Another was to deprive subareas of agricultural economics other than farm management of the contributions of production economics. Both by neglecting or, conversely, somewhat arrogantly attempting to dominate such other multidisciplinary subfields of agricultural economics as resource (land) economics, marketing, policy, finance, cooperatives, and economic development, specialized agricultural production economists caused persons working in these other areas to neglect or react adversely to production economics. Resource economists now have a separate association that meets jointly with the AAEA. Kelso and others write of resource economics as being a separate discipline. In marketing, engineering production relationships and the industrial organization approach fail to benefit from production economics as much as they probably could. Policy analysis, too, has probably been deprived of much of what production economics could have contributed had it not been so focused on and identified with farm management. The same is true for the study of agricultural finance and cooperatives. As third world agricultural work uses almost all of agricultural economics (and more), it is also constrained.

As pointed out in my 1963 review, the initial impact of production economics on traditional farm management was to make farm management more problem oriented. But that impact was ephemeral as (a) the positivistic orientation of production economics led to neglect of the study of values on which the definition and solution of practical problems depend, (b) a specialized subdiscipline such as production economics was unable to provide full intellectual support for defining and solving multidisciplinary practical problems and, (c) intriguing new techniques in economics developed rapidly. Positivism seriously constrains the ability to research values and, hence, to define and solve problems. Even conditional normativism yields only rather arbitrary definitions and solutions of problems, while the other variant of logical positivism, Parieto optimality, yields mainly solutions to problems the market can solve as well without the assistance of economists. Specialization of production economists on a subpart of a single discipline — economics — made it difficult to maintain an interest in the various multidisciplinary dimensions of practical problems. Further, the difficulty of maintaining a focus on problems was made more acute by the rapid development of new and intriguing techniques hardly existing when Heady's book was written. It became easier and

easier for production economists to become subdisciplinary and technique oriented and to neglect multidisciplinary problem solving work
as attention focused on Cobb-Douglas analysis, linear programming,
input/output analyses, expected utility analysis, and frontier production functions. However, it must be noted that this tendency was not
confined to production economists or, for that matter, even to agricultural economists who were generally implicated by Brinegar, Bachman, and Southworth. In this period, academia and its administrators became enamored with disciplinary accomplishments and
publications in peer-reviewed journals (the more disciplinary the better) that they became the road to promotion and distinction.

Since 1963 there has also been a reduced emphasis by agricultural production economists on empirical work. Production economic
theory has become more axiomatized and more analytic. The expe-
riential meaning of undefined primitive terms has been neglected as
has the synthetic descriptive knowledge resulting from using primitive
terms to convert abstract analytic systems into descriptive (synthetic)
knowledge. Again, what has happened with respect to agricultural
production economics is part of a wider pattern involving all of agricultural economics, general economics, academia in general, and society at large. Leontief (1982) and Mini, for examples, have deplored
the neglect of the empirical by economists. Earlier, in his 1971 AEA
presidential address, Leontief complimented agricultural economists
for their empirical work; now, it is doubtful if he would repeat his
compliment.

An unfortunate consequence of neglecting empirical work is that
theoretical formulations go untested and, hence, unproved. Empirical
testing is part of the self-pruning, healing, and improving capacity of
science. Production economics has several analytical developments in
need of testing and, perhaps, pruning and healing that I have listed
elsewhere (Johnson, forthcoming) and there are more. Those I have
listed include (a) the currently used and highly questionable distinction between technical and economic efficiency, (b) the concepts of
risk preference and aversion as part of the expected utility analysis of
risk, (c) the concept of macro-production functions and applications
of duality theory that either assume the validity of such functions or
use empirically questionable estimates of them, and (d) the concept of
frontier production functions. As Leontief and Mini stress, the short-

age of empirical work to quantify and test such abstractions is highly regrettable and hardly in keeping with Heady's empiricism.

The difficulties noted above are widespread. They are part of the "modernism" attacked by McCloskey in his critical works (1983, 1985) on rhetoric in economics. They are also considered by McClennen in his excellent review entitled "Rational Choice and Public Policy" and by Cooter and Rappoport in their article entitled "Were the Ordinalists Wrong?"

There are three other current difficulties more specific to agricultural production economics and/or farm management. They involve (a) managerial theory and the empirical study of managerial processes; (b) the dynamics of technical, institutional, and human change; and (c) the dynamics of capital investment and disinvestment, growth (net investment), deterioration (net disinvestment), and utilization. Though Heady's book gives little attention to these difficulties, putting his book in perspective requires that they be listed and briefly discussed.

Current theoretical work on managerial processes is highly specialized on the expected utility hypothesis to the neglect of optimization vis-à-vis problem definition; the acquisition of value and value-free knowledge (learning); analysis; decision-making rules beyond the expected utility hypothesis; performance of the administrative and executive function by managers; and, finally, the bearing of responsibility for actions taken. This broader, more complete view of management needs to be researched theoretically and empirically not only for the sake of farm management but for the sakes of agribusiness and public management as well (Johnson 1977).

Schultz (1956, 1958, 1959, 1960, 1971), Hayami and Ruttan (1970a, 1971), Ruttan, Turran and Hayami, and several other University of Chicago and related scholars have focused on the limiting constraints of static assumptions vis-à-vis the state of the arts, human capacity, and institutional structures. The agricultural production economics movement has been criticized for failing to deal endogenously with these three dynamic driving forces affecting agricultural production. The criticisms were valid, and they have been followed by the development of rather self-evident, induced-change hypotheses with respect to technology, human capital, and institutions. These hypotheses extend the concept of the market to the public sector — to legislators, government executives, and politicians. Empirical work has sustained these hypotheses by explaining previously unexplained technical, institutional, and human changes and, with the help of such explanations, previously unexplained changes in agricultural production. Fine, excellent progress has been made—yet not everything has been explained, including the roles of curiosity as it drives technical researchers and inventors; zeal, the quest for fame, and willingness to sacrifice to help underdogs that drive institutional reformers; and pride, self-identification, customs, attitudes, and the like as they influence the development of human capacity. Changes in technology, institutions, and human capacity are multidisciplinary in ways that go beyond markets (however broadly defined) to disciplines other than economics. Our work is not yet done if we are to understand fully the multidisciplinary dimensions of the generation and utilization of these three driving forces for agricultural production.

Traditional man-made capital and natural resources also contribute to agricultural production and are affected by net investment and disinvestment in them. Serious problems exist even if we have made considerable progress in understanding investment, disinvestment, numerous opportunity cost concepts, and user costs. As a profession we failed to spot and do enough about the overinvestment that has brought about the current farm and farm credit crises—the 1920s indicate that the causes run deeper and include more than the price support programs many now so facilely blame for our surpluses. At a theoretical level, user cost theory is not well enough developed to explain adequately how variations in the rate at which services are extracted from durable resources affect production. Many of us fail to question and even preach, despite our Parieto optimality, that the non-Parieto-optimal losses imposed on farmers and others by the operation of markets among imperfectly informed participants are "for the good of all concerned." The supply and factor demand functions used in many policy analyses are still conceived to be reversible and unshifted by investments, disinvestments and changes in the rate at which services are extracted from durables. Correspondingly, our linear programs do not vary service extraction rates for durables endogenously and, when we try to make them do so, will not solve on our computers. There is much work still to be done.

On the value side, too many production economists and others stick to logical positivism and its variants. Even pragmatic institutionalists sometimes join the positivists. Yet, logical positivism is now treated in the past tense by many philosophers. In the past ten years there have been at least ten national conferences on values in agriculture and on agro-ethics, and a national effort is being sponsored by the National Association of State Universities and Land-Grant Colleges (NASULGC) and the National Association of State Colleges of Agriculture and Renewable Resources (NASCARR) to develop undergraduate teaching materials on agro-ethics. It is increasingly respectable for economists to research values and, it can be argued, it is possible to do so in an objective manner. Perhaps it is time for more production economists to concede something to the pragmatic institutionalists and, indeed, to go beyond pragmatic institutionalism to other normative philosophies for methodological guidance in researching values for use in defining and solving problems solvable only with market interventions.

Space does permit an adequate review of how the difficulties mentioned above are being handled in the current crop of texts pertaining to agricultural production economics, agricultural policy, marketing, farm management, resource economics, agricultural development. Such a review is needed. I believe it would reveal important adjustments — spotty and incomplete, perhaps, but nonetheless progress that builds on Heady's major contribution and serves to alleviate the difficulties that have arisen in the agricultural production economics movement of which Heady's book was, and still is, such an important part.

IN CONCLUSION

Since 1963, agricultural production economics has made major contributions and much progress along lines laid out by Heady in his magnificent book. These contributions and progress have created many problems and difficulties unforeseen by Heady and the colleagues (including me) who worked with him in the post–World War II agricultural production economics movement. We should have expected this, the question of whether we did or did not being a different matter. These difficulties have arisen partially as a result of success of agricultural production economists and partly as a result of the overall societal and academic environment in which they have worked since 1952. Were Heady still working among us, he would have just reasons to be proud of his accomplishments. All of us have ample reasons to be proud of his book and his great accomplishments. As for the difficulties and problems, they present opportunities for the members of the generation that succeeds Earl Heady and the rest of the generation of production economists who took part in the post–World War II agricultural production economics movement.

Glenn L. Johnson
Michigan State University

NOTE

1. Though this review has benefitted from much-appreciated suggestions and criticisms from Larry Connor, James Bonnen, Allan Schmid, and Patrick Madden, the author remains solely responsible for it.

REFERENCES

Arrow, Kenneth J. *Social Choice and Individual Values.* New York; John Wiley & Sons, 1951.

Black, John D. *Introduction to Production Economics.* New York: Henry Holt & Co., 1926.

Black, J. D., M. Clawson, C. R. Sayre, and W. W. Wilcox. *Farm Management.* New York: Macmillan Co., 1947.

Boulding, Kenneth. *Economic Analysis.* New York: Harper & Row, 1948.

_____. "Economics as a Moral Science." *Amer. Econ. Rev.* 59(1969):1–12.

Brinegar, G. K., K. L. Bachman, and H.M. Southworth. "Reorientations in Research in Agricultural Economics." *J. Farm Econ.* 41(1959):600–619.

Carlson, Sune. *A Study in the Pure Theory of Production.* London: P. S. King, 1939.

Cooter, R., and P. Rappoport. "Were the Ordinalists Wrong About Welfare Economics?" *J. Econ. Lit.* 22(1984):207–53.

Ezekiel, Mordecai. *Methods of Correlation Analysis.* New York: John Wiley & Sons, 1930.

Fox, Karl A., and D. Gale Johnson, eds. *Readings in the Economics of Agriculture,* vol. 13. Homewood, IL: Richard D. Irwin, 1969.

Friedman, Milton, and L. J. Savage. "The Utility Analysis of Choices Involving Risks." *J. Polit. Econ.* 56(1948):279–304.

Hart, A. G. "Risk, Uncertainty and the Unprofitability of Compounding Probabilities." *Studies in Mathematical Economics and Econometrics.* Chicago:University of Chicago Press, 1942.

Glenn L. Johnson   191

Hayami, Y., and V. W. Ruttan. *Agricultural Development, An International Perspective.*
Baltimore: John Hopkins University Press, 1971.
_____. "Agricultural Productivity Differences Among Countries." *Amer. Econ. Rev.*
60(1970a):895–911.
_____. "Factor Prices and Technical Change in Agricultural Development: The
United States and Japan, 1880–1960." *J. Polit. Econ.* 78(1970b):115–41.
Johnson, Glenn L. "Agricultural Economics, Production Economics and the Field of
Farm Management." *J. Farm Econ.* 38(1957):441–50.
_____. "Contributions of Economists to a Rational Decision-Making Process in the
Field of Agricultural Policy." *Decision-Making and Agriculture,* ed. T. Dams and K.
E. Hunt, pp. 15–46. Oxford: Agricultural Economics Institute, 1977.
_____. "Philosophic Foundations of Agricultural Economics Thought." *A Survey of
Agricultural Economics Literature,* vol. IV, ed. Lee R. Martin. Minneapolis: University of Minnesota Press, forthcoming.
_____. *Research Methodology for Economists,* New York: Macmillan Co., 1986.
_____. "Small Farms in a Changing World." *Proceedings,* 1981 farming systems research symposium, "Small Farms in a Changing World: Prospects for the Eighties." Kansas State University Pap. No. 2, pp. 7–28, 1982.
_____. "Stress on Production Economics." *Aust. J. Agr. Econ.* 7(1963):12–26.
Kelso, Maurice M. "National Resource Economics: The Upsetting Discipline." *Amer.
J. Agr. Econ.* 59(1977):814–23.
Knight, Frank C. *Risk, Uncertainty and Profit.* New York: Houghton Mifflin Co., 1946
(originally published in 1921).
Koopmans, T. C., ed. *Activity Analysis of Production and Allocation.* New York: John
Wiley & Sons, 1951.
Leontief, Wassily. "Academic Economics." *Science* 217(1982):104–7.
_____. "Theoretical Assumptions and Non-Observed Facts." *Amer. Econ. Rev.*
61(1971):1–7.
MacFarlane, David D. "Review of *Economics of Agricultural Production and Resource Use,*
by Earl Heady." *J. Farm Econ.* 35(1953):444–45.
McClennen, Edward F. "Rational Choice and Public Policy." *Social Theory and Practice*
9(1983):335–79.
McCloskey, Donald N. "The Rhetoric of Economics." *J. Econ. Lit.* 21(1983):481–517.
_____. *The Rhetoric of Economics.* Madison: University of Wisconsin Press, 1985.
Mini, P. V. *Philosophy and Economics.* Gainesville: University of Florida Press, 1974.
Myrdal, Gunnar. *The American Dilemma.* New York: Harper Brothers, 1944.
Nicol, Kenneth J., Somnuk Sriplung, and Earl O. Heady, eds. *Agricultural Development
Planning in Thailand.* Ames: Iowa State University Press, 1982.
Ramaratnam, S. Sri. "An Overview of the Holistic Farm Management Research and
Extension Programs with Emphasis on Past U.S. Farm and Home Programs
and Current Farming Systems Research in the Developing Countries." Dept.
Agr. Econ. Plan B Paper, Michigan State University, 1981.
Reder, Melvin W. *Studies in the Theory of Welfare Economics.* New York: Columbia
University Press, 1947.
Ruttan, V. W. "Induced Technical and Institutional Change and the Future of Agriculture." *The Future of Agriculture,* Papers and Reports of the Fifteenth International Conference of Agricultural Economists, San Paulo, Brazil, 19–30 Aug.
1973, pp. 35–52. Oxford: Alden Press, 1974.

Ruttan V. W., and Y. Hayami. "Strategies for Agricultural Development." *Food Res. Inst. Stud.* 11(1972):129–48.

Samuelson, Paul. *Foundation of Economic Analysis.* Cambridge: Harvard University Press, 1948.

Schultz, T. W. "Capital Formation by Education." *J. Polit. Econ.* 67(1960):571–83.

————. *Investment in Human Capital.* New York: Free Press, 1971.

————. "Investment in Man: An Economist's View." *Proceedings and Debates of the 86th Congress,* 1st Sess. no. 169, vol. 106, 5 Oct. 1959.

————. "Output-Input Relationships Revisited." *J. Farm Econ.* 40:(1958):924–32.

————. "Reflections on Agricultural Production, Output and Supply." *J. Farm Econ.* 38(1956):746–62.

Stigler, George J. *Production and Distribution Theories.* New York: Macmillan Co., 1948.

vonNeumann, J., and O. Morgenstern. *Theory of Games and Economic Behavior,* 2nd ed. Princeton: Princeton University Press, 1947.

193-97 (handwritten)

B31 (handwritten)

A Personal Synopsis *eds*

EARL O. HEADY

Born: January 25, 1916, to Jessie (Banks) and Orel C. Heady, Champion, Nebraska. Raised on a Chase County, Nebraska Farm. Graduated from Chase County High School, Imperial, Nebraska. B.S., University of Nebraska, 1938. M.S., University of Nebraska, 1939. Ph.D., Iowa State University, 1945. Attended University of Chicago, 1941. Employed by the Federal Land Bank of Omaha 1939–1940. Professor of Economics; Charles F. Curtiss Distinguished Professor of Agriculture; Director of the Center for Agricultural and Rural Development from 1957–1983. Became faculty member of Iowa State University in 1940. Professor Emeritus of Economics, 1983–1987.

In 1941 married Marian Ruth Hoppert. Three children: Marilyn Kling, Macomb, Illinois; Stephen Heady, Beaverton, Oregon; Barbara Heady, Ames, Iowa. Three grandchildren.

Died: August 20, 1987
Buried: Iowa State University Cemetery

Honorary Degrees

Dr.Sc., University of Nebraska, 1960; honorary member, Hungarian Academy of Science, 1964; Dr.Sc. Honoris Causa, University of Upsalla and Agricultural College of Sweden, member, Royal Swedish Academy of Science, 1974; Doctor Honoris Causa, Agricultural University of Debrecen (Hungary), 1979; Doctor Honoris Causa, Warsaw Agricultural University, 1979; honorary member of the Soviet Academy of Agricultural Sciences, 1982.

Academic and Professional Honors

Certificate of superior scholarship (upper 3 percent of graduating class), University of Nebraska; Alpha Zeta, Gamma Sigma Delta, Pi Kappa Phi; Sigma Xi; Phi Beta Kappa; Social Science Research Council Award, 1950–53; American Agricultural Economics Association Award for outstanding research, 1949, 1952, 1956, 1957, 1959, 1973, 1974, 1975, 1976, 1980; named first Distinguished Professor at Iowa State University, 1956; Fellow, Advanced Center for Behavioral Science, 1960–1961; Iowa Gamma Sigma Delta award for outstanding service to agriculture, 1962; American Agricultural Editor's Annual National Award for Outstanding and Distinguished Service to American Agriculture, 1965; Iowa State University Press Award for best book by a staff member; Fellow, American Agricultural Economics Association, 1963; Fellow, Econometrics Society 1965; Fellow, American Statistical Association, 1966; Fellow, American Association for Advancement of Science 1966; Fellow, American Academy of Arts and Sciences, 1977; vice-president of Canadian Agricultural Economics Association; permanent chairman, East-West Seminars for Agricultural Economists; Des Moines Chamber of Commerce World Citizenship Award for distinguished service to other countries, 1974; KSO Great Country Award, 1974; Gamma Sigma Delta Annual International Award for Distinguished Service to Agriculture, 1975; Iowa State University Alumni Association Faculty Citation for Outstanding and Inspiring Service, 1977; Wilton Park Award, 1977; the Browning Award and medal by the American Society of Agronomy, 1977; American Agricultural Economics Association Special Award, 1978; Iowa State University Henry A. Wallace Award for Distinguished Service to Agriculture, 1978; Rockefeller Study and Conference Center Scholar-in-Residence, Bellagio, Italy, 1983, Excellence in Agriculture Award, National Farmland Appraisers Association, 1984; and miscellaneous others.

National Committees

Member, White House Committee on Domestic Affairs; member, Research Advisory Committee, United States Agency for International Development; member, advisory committee, United States

State Department on World Food Programs; member, advisory board, Economics Institute; member, advisory board, Rural Community Assistance Program of the Association of State Universities and Land-Grant Colleges — Office for Advancement of Public Negro Colleges; member, Social Science Research Council Panel on Research Methods in Agricultural Economics; member, University of Chicago Seminar on Agricultural Efficiency; member, Commission of Human Settlements; member, American Economic Association Council of Speakers; member, National Coordinating Committee, Regional Centers for Rural Development; member, Advisory Committee Agricultural Policy Institute, North Carolina State University; member, Planning Committee, National Farm Policy Institute; member, International Committee, Editorial Council and Awards Committee; member, American Association of Agricultural Economists; member, Agricultural and Land Committees, National Planning Association; chairman, Office of Technology Assessment of United States Congress Panel on Land Productivity; member, National Academy of Science, National Research Council on Food Production and Maintenance of Soil Productivity; director of Modeling Committee for Analysis of Resources Conservation Act by United States Department of Agriculture; miscellaneous others.

Other Professional Experiences

Visiting professor at Harvard University, University of Illinois, University of California at Berkeley, North Carolina State University, Stanford University; consultant to the President's Materials Policy Commission; consultant to National Food and Fiber Commission; consultant to the National Water Commission; visiting lecturer for the American Economics Association; consultant to the Esso Research Foundation; consultant to the Organization for Economic Cooperation and Development (Paris); consultant to the Food and Agriculture Organization, United Nations Development Fund; consultant to the Government of India on research and graduate training programs; consultant to Ministry of Agriculture and Ministry of Coordination of Greece; consultant to Ministry of Agriculture, Kingdom of Ethiopia; consultant to the Ministry of Agriculture and Water, Kingdom of Saudi Arabia; consultant to the Ministry of Agriculture,

Kingdom of Thailand; consultant to the Ministry of Agriculture, Romania; consultant to the Ministry of Agriculture, Mexico; consultant to the Ministry of Agriculture and Fisheries, Government of Portugal; adviser to the Minister of Agriculture, Egypt; consultant to the Hungarian Agricultural Economics Research Institute; consultant to the Agricultural Marketing Service of the USDA; consultant to the Tennessee Valley Authority; consultant to Doxiades Associates, Athens, Greece; consultant to the Stanford Research Institute; consultant to Experience Incorporated; consultant to Acres Research and Planning Limited; consultant and research collaborator for International Institute of Applied Systems Analysis, Austria; director, Iowa State University–Ford Foundation Program for Graduate Training and Research at National College of Agriculture, Mexico; consultant to United States Office of the Secretary of Agriculture; panel member, Office of Technology Assessment, United States House of Congress; consultant to Ford Foundation on East Europe and Latin American Programs; director of the Iowa State University–AID–Ministry of Agriculture Sector Planning Project in Thailand; director, Iowa State University–AID–Bureau of Planning, Technical Assistant Program in Indonesia; lecturer to many United States and foreign universities and research institutes; miscellaneous others.

Foreign Travel and Work Experience

Canada, Costa Rica, Mexico, Argentina, Ethiopia, Columbia, Nigeria, Turkey, Egypt, Greece, Yugoslavia, Czechoslovakia, Romania, Hungary, Poland, Russia, Italy, Switzerland, Austria, Germany, England, Spain, Portugal, France, Denmark, Norway, Sweden, Belgium, Netherlands, India, Pakistan, Philippines, South Africa, Japan, Thailand, Lebanon, Indonesia, Australia, Iran, Saudi Arabia, Taiwan, Guatemala.

Publications

Author and co-author of 26 books and more than 750 journal articles, research bulletins, and monographs.

Listing in Scientific, Professional, and Other Directories

Who's Who in America, Who's Who in the World, Who's Who in the Midwest, World's Who's Who of Scientists from Antiquity to the Present, American Men of Science, American Directory of Scholars, American Economic Association, American Agricultural Economics Association and others.